Foreword

The Ulster Architectural Heritage Society is pleased to publish **A DIRECTORY OF FUNDS FOR HISTORIC BUILDINGS IN NORTHERN IRELAND** as part of the Buildings at Risk programme which it carries out in association with the Environment and Heritage Service of the Department of the Environment, Northern Ireland.

We are most grateful to the Department for their on-going support which they have given this programme for seven years. During that time we have published six *Buildings at Risk* catalogues, and three editions of the *Directory of Traditional Building Skills*, not to mention the conference papers from *'Bliss or Blitz?'* Forthcoming publications include another *Buildings at Risk* catalogue containing the Conference papers relating to 'Buildings at Risk: S O S: Some Options and Solutions' held in October 1999. The Society values highly its relationship with the Service and its staff over these highly productive years.

These previous publications have highlighted buildings, which are in need of a new future and have provided information about accessing the appropriate skilled professional for help with their restoration.

This directory provides guidance on how to find help to pay for the work. It is a wide-ranging list of potential funding bodies. Although there are other funding directories for the arts generally, this is the first for the repair and restoration of historic buildings. It is important however, to note that the funding scene is changing rapidly. Not only will Northern Ireland loose its Category 1 status within the European Union, but all the European grants are currently under discussion and the new programmes for 2000-2006 will be announced in the new year. The breadth and extent of the Directory will encourage readers to think hard and imaginatively about where they might find financial help.

The Ulster Architectural Heritage Society is very grateful to Hilary Weir, Secretary of the Architectural Heritage Fund based in London, for extensive support and access to their funding database. This directory has been compiled by Harriet Devlin, the Society's Buildings at Risk Officer, who, as in so many other areas has done so with efficiency, enthusiasm and hard work.

We trust that the Funding Directory for Historic Buildings in Northern Ireland, made widely available at no cost, will prove another effective step towards helping to preserve Northern Ireland's important built heritage.

Peter O. Marlow
Chairman

Introduction

The purpose of this guide is to bring together the information on various sources of funding for historic building in Northern Ireland into one user-friendly resource. For potential restorers of historic buildings access to up to date information about relevant sources of finance has always been a huge headache. Some sources are fairly straight forward, but others are not easy to find or to understand. It is hoped that easier access to information about funds will encourage more individuals and groups to consider undertaking projects to repair and restore Northern Ireland's built heritage.

A huge debt of thanks is owed to several individuals and institutions whose help was invaluable to the writing of this document. Firstly to Hilary Weir of the Architectural Heritage Fund whose own Directory of Funds for England and Wales, 1998 & 1999 was not only the inspiration but also the template for this volume. Her generosity and unstinting encouragement were the catalyst for getting this directory published. Secondly to Chris Colville and Elaine Grey who compiled 'A Directory of Sources of Financial Assistance for Historic Buildings in Northern Ireland' for the Environment & Heritage Service in 1997. This was never published, but the manuscript has been an invaluable source of information. In turn, the grandmother of them all was Mary Miers pioneering work for the Scottish Civic Trust in 1991 that provided the first specialised funding directory for historic buildings in the British Isles.

This Directory is lamentably incomplete in that one of the major sources of financial assistance for buildings in Northern Ireland has been access to the many various strands of funds from Europe. It has been published at a cross roads in funding, the European funding measures 1994-1999 have all been allocated and a short hiatus will ensue until the new measures 2000-2006 are agreed and come on stream , which is anticipated to be by late spring 2000. In the section on European Funding (p. 20) addresses are given for further information.

It is obvious that sources of funding are constantly changing. For example the duration of the Townscape Heritage Initiative that will have promised over £8 million of Heritage Lottery money to the most needy town and village centres by the end of 1999 is not certain. It will achieve an enormous impact on the preservation and appearance of many conservation areas in the province, but only one further bidding round, in 2000 is confirmed. To keep abreast of the changing funds, the Directory will have to be updated on a regular basis.

WORK TO HISTORIC BUILDINGS : Things to think about

1. Statutory Consents

The local Planning Divisional Office should be the first port of call for anyone contemplating a project involving an historic building, to ascertain whether listed building consent is required as well as planning permission.

2. Value Added Tax

Value Added Tax is a wide ranging tax levied at the standard rate of 17 1/2% on most goods and services. There is a certain amount of confusion regarding the application of VAT and work to listed buildings. Whilst new build is zero-rated, currently works of repair and maintenance are standard rated at 17 1/2% but under certain conditions approved ALTERATIONS may be zero-rated.

Approved alterations to listed buildings and scheduled monuments may qualify for zero rating if:
- they are statutorily listed (unlisted buildings in Conservation Areas do NOT qualify).
- listed building consent from the Environment & Heritage Service has been sought and approved. **n.b.** Listed building consent does not automatically make the work zero-rated. Listed churches do not require listed building consent for the purpose of VAT relief on alterations.
- the building must be a protected building, that is, a listed building that is or will be, on completion of the alterations, a dwelling, a relevant residential building, or a relevant charitable building.

- the work does not constitute repairs or maintenance.
- mixed work may be apportioned between qualifying zero-rated alterations and standard rated elements.
- the work is undertaken by a VAT registered builder. DIY work will not qualify, nor will VAT relief apply if the materials are bought for the builder. However if applicants are VAT registered themselves VAT may be recovered.

If a relevant housing association (that is a registered social landlord, or a registered housing association) is converting a building from non residential use to a dwelling services may be zero-rated.

Items that can be zero rated:
- the services supplied in carrying out an approved alteration to a protected building or qualifying building.
- the services supplied in carrying out an approved alteration to a protected building which is a qualifying building, to convert it into a dwelling.
- the building materials used in the course of carrying out approved alterations.

There has been a vigorous campaign from the Joint Committee of Amenity Societies who are currently lobbying the Treasury for a review of the VAT legislation, as it obviously is a very substantial added cost to most restoration projects, and runs contrary to ideas of sustainable development.

For further information, as well as advice on these and other concessions that might be relevant the local VAT office should always be contacted:

HM Customs & Excise
Business Advice Unit
Custom House
Queen's Square
Belfast
BT1 3EU
Tel 0345 125730
Fax 01232 562972

The explanatory Notice 708 VAT: Buildings and construction is very useful

3. Feasibility Studies
If a project is of any significant scale it will benefit from some form of feasibility study. The Heritage Lottery Fund encourages a conservation plan and/or a business plan to be drawn up for large projects. This is an added cost to consider, though there are a few sources of grant that are included in the Directory.

4. Public Support
The preservation of historic buildings is not always at the top of the agenda of some local councils or of some private owners, particularly in the case of Buildings at Risk. Public support for the restoration of a building can be very useful in raising awareness of the importance of the building(s). The presence of a local campaign, or demonstration of public concern can sometimes assist the application for funds, as the perception of public benefit from funded projects is increasingly important.

5. Applying to charitable trusts
It is unusual for funding bodies to offer grants for work that has already begun, therefore it is very important to plan well in advance, and realise that applying for funding can take a very long time.

If the project is likely to need financial support, the Directory should be consulted and there is the possibility of advice from the Northern Ireland Council for Voluntary Action, N.I.C.V.A. to find appropriate funding sources. Make sure that all the information required by the source (e.g. a copy of the audited accounts), is available and that a realistic budget for the project is provided.

The application should be tailored to the needs of the trust being approached. Duplicated mail shot and applications by fax or e-mail should be avoided. It is important to be specific about the requirements, but applicants should be prepared to apply to several sources of funding as many charitable trusts only have limited resources. Indeed many funders now require partnership arrangements whereby funds from several sources are amalgamated to provide maximum monies for the project.

As it may become necessary to apply to the same fund again, it is advisable to establish good relations with the funders, to keep records of everything and too keep the funders informed on the progress of the project. An expression of thanks will not go amiss.

6. Technical advice

The repair and restoration of historic buildings requires specialist conservation skills. Many funders may make the issue of grant contingent on employing trained conservation architects to draw up the scheme, and contractors with experience of working with historic buildings. The *Directory of Traditional Building Skills*, available free of charge on collection from the Ulster Architectural Heritage Society, is a very useful guide to skilled professionals within Northern Ireland . Technical notes on various aspects of remedial works to listed buildings are readily available from the Environment & Heritage Service.

We hope that this Directory will simplify the funding minefield for all potential restorers.

Harriet Devlin
1 October 1999

How to use the Directory

Organisation

The Directory is divided into sections by categories of funding source (see contents page). Within each section, entries are arranged alphabetically by source.

The Index is the quickest way to find a source if you know its name.

The 'Quick Reference Guide' (see p.xi) is designed to help you establish at a glance the source(s) most likely to be relevant to your project. Arranged in section order, it is in effect an itemised table of contents and summary of each entry.

Information Provided

We have tried to provide sufficient information to enable users to decide whether a project is eligible in principle for funds from a particular source; to flag key points in the application procedure and to enable users to get in touch with the source to obtain further information.

Accuracy

We have made every effort to ensure that the entries are entirely accurate. Every funding source was asked to review its entry in draft. The most up to date information available was used up to the end of September 1999. In order to maintain accuracy it is anticipated that the Directory will be regularly updated.

The new package of funding sources form Europe (see section B) is currently under discussion and the exact programmes have not yet been announced. It is anticipated that the programmes and their means of delivery will be operational by Spring 2000. It is advised that for further information applicants consult:

Department of Finance & Personnel
Rosepark House
Upper Newtownards Road
Belfast
Tel: 01232 520400

The Northern Ireland Council for Voluntary Action, NICVA is also currently compiling a directory of sources of funding available to the voluntary and community sector, named Grant Tracker. The staff are very willing to assist potential applicants. Contact:

Jayne Blayney or Sylvia Gordon
NICVA,
127 Ormeau Road,
Belfast BT7 1SH
Tel: 01232 321224
Fax: 01232 438350
e-mail: nicva@nicva.org

Standard Form of Entries

We hope that the standard form for each entry is clear and easily understood.

Amount
The amount normally given to a successful applicant.

Form of Payment
Whether one-off or in installments, and at what stage of the project the payment is likely to be made.

Size of Fund
The assets and /or capital on which the source can draw to fund its programme(s) of assistance. The aim is to enable the user to judge the likelihood of receiving funding.

Very small	assets/capital of less than £100,000
Small	assets/capital between £100,000 and £500,000
Medium	assets/capital between £500,000 and £1.5 million
Large	assets/capital between £1.5 million and £5 million
Very Large	assets/capital over £5 million

Application Form?
Whether an application form exists and if not, how to apply. What material to submit. Whether all applicants are acknowledged, whether unsuccessful applicants are notified.

Timetable
The timescale within which an application normally proceeds to a decision; the frequency of meetings and how far in advance an application must be made.

Notes
Any information not included in the main body of the text.

#
Nothing pertinent to enter against a particular heading.

N/A
Not available.

A somewhat shorter version of the standard form has been deployed in Section E.

QUICK REFERENCE GUIDE

Ulster Architectural Heritage Society

Section	Name	Programme	Geographical Area	Size of Fund	Charities Only	Secular Buildings	Religious Buildings	Feasibility Studies	Page
A 1	CUSTOMS AND EXCISE	Landfill Tax Credit Scheme	UK	Very large		Yes	Yes		2
A 2	DEPARTMENT OF ECONOMIC DEVELOPMENT	Domestic Energy Efficiency Scheme: Home Insulation Grants	Northern Ireland	Medium		Yes			3
A 3	DEPARTMENT OF THE ENVIRONMENT	Conservation Area Grants	Northern Ireland			Yes	Yes		4
A 4	DEPARTMENT OF THE ENVIRONMENT: Environment & Heritage Service	Historic Buildings Grant	Northern Ireland	Large		Yes	Yes		5
A 5	DEPARTMENT OF THE ENVIRONMENT	Scheduled Historic Monuments	Northern Ireland	Very small		Yes	Yes		6
A 6	DEPARTMENT OF THE ENVIRONMENT	Urban Development Grant UDG		Large		Yes	Yes		7
A 7	ENERGY EFFICIENCY ADVICE CENTRE	Cavity Wall grant	Northern Ireland	Small		Yes			8
A 8	ENERGY EFFICIENCY ADVICE CENTRE	Condensing boiler grant	UK	Small		Yes			9
A 9	NATIONAL HERITAGE MEMORIAL FUND		UK	Medium		Yes	Yes		10
A 10	NORTHERN IRELAND HOUSING EXECUTIVE	Home Improvement grants: Common Parts Grants	Northern Ireland	Medium		Yes			11
A 11	NORTHERN IRELAND HOUSING EXECUTIVE	Home Improvement grants: Disabled Facilities Grants	Northern Ireland	Medium		Yes			12
A 12	NORTHERN IRELAND HOUSING EXECUTIVE	Home Improvement grants: Houses in Multiple Occupation (HMO)	Northern Ireland	Medium		Yes			13
A 13	NORTHERN IRELAND HOUSING EXECUTIVE	Home Improvement grants: Group Repair	Northern Ireland	Medium		Yes			14
A 14	NORTHERN IRELAND HOUSING EXECUTIVE	Home Improvement grants: Minor Works Assistance	Northern Ireland	Medium		Yes			15
A 15	NORTHERN IRELAND HOUSING EXECUTIVE	Home Improvement grants: Renovation Grants	Northern Ireland	Medium		Yes			16
A 16	NORTHERN IRELAND HOUSING EXECUTIVE	Home Improvement grants: Repairs Grants	Northern Ireland	Medium		Yes			17
B 1	EUROPEAN UNION	Culture 2000 (provisional title)	EU Member	Very large		Yes	Yes		22
B 2	EUROPEAN UNION	European Regional Development Fund	Northern Ireland			Yes	Yes		23
B 3	INTERNATIONAL FUND FOR IRELAND	Disadvantaged Areas Initiative: CERS and CRISP	Designated settlements in Northern Ireland	Large	Yes	Yes	Yes		24

Section	Name	Programme	Geographical Area	Size of Fund	Charities Only	Secular Buildings	Religious Buildings	Feasibility Studies	Page
E 1	ALLCHURCHES TRUST LIMITED		UK	Small	Yes	Yes	Yes		46
E 2	LORD BARNBY'S FOUNDATION		UK	Large	Yes	Yes	Yes		46
E 3	THE BEAVERBROOK FOUNDATION		UK	Large	Yes		Yes		47
E 4	WILLIAM ADLINGTON CADBURY CHARITABLE TRUST		UK	Small	Yes	Yes	Yes		47
E 5	CHARITIES AID FOUNDATION	Investors in Society	UK	Large		Yes	Yes		48
E 6	THE CHASE CHARITY		UK	Large	Yes	Yes	Yes		48
E 7	THE CLOTHWORKERS' FOUNDATION		UK	Very large	Yes	Yes			49
E 8	THE JOHN S COHEN FOUNDATION		UK	Large	Yes	Yes			49
E 9	ENKALON FOUNDATION		Northern Ireland	Very small	Yes	Yes	Yes		50
E 10	THE ALAN EVANS MEMORIAL TRUST		UK	Medium	Yes	Yes	Yes		50
E 11	THE ESMÉE FAIRBAIRN CHARITABLE TRUST		UK	Very large	Yes	Yes	Yes		51
E 12	THE FERMANAGH TRUST		Co Fermanagh	Very small		Yes	Yes		51
E 13	FORD OF BRITAIN TRUST		UK	Small	Yes	Yes			52
E 14	J PAUL GETTY JR CHARITABLE TRUST		UK	Very large	Yes	Yes			52
E 15	G C GIBSON TRUST		UK	Large	Yes		Yes		53
E 16	THE GLAZIERS' TRUST		UK	Very small		Yes	Yes		53
E 17	THE GROCERS' CHARITY		UK	Small	Yes	Yes	Yes		54
E 18	IDLEWILD TRUST		UK	Large	Yes	Yes	Yes		54
E 19	THE IRELAND FUNDS		Ireland	Very large		Yes	Yes		55
E 20	THE IRISH LANDMARK TRUST		Ireland	Medium					55
E 21	THE IRONMONGERS' CHARITABLE FUND		UK	Small	Yes	Yes	Yes		56
E 22	LECHE TRUST		UK	Small		Yes	Yes		56

Section	Name	Programme	Geographical Area	Size of Fund	Charities Only	Secular Buildings	Religious Buildings	Feasibility Studies	Page
E 23	THE HELEN ISABELLA McMORRAN CHARITABLE TRUST		UK	Medium	Yes		Yes		57
E 24	THE MANIFOLD CHARITABLE TRUST		UK	Very large	Yes	Yes	Yes		57
E 25	MERCERS' COMPANY		UK	Medium	Yes	Yes			58
E 26	THE ESME MITCHELL TRUST		Ireland	Small	Yes	Yes	Yes		58
E 27	THE PILGRIM TRUST		UK	Very large	Yes	Yes	Yes		59
E 28	THE ROTHSCHILD FOUNDATION		UK	Very large	Yes	Yes	Yes		59
E 29	SAINSBURY FAMILY CHARITABLE TRUSTS		UK	Very large	Yes	Yes	Yes		60
E 30	SHELL BETTER BRITAIN CAMPAIGN	Community Projects Fund	UK	Small		Yes	Yes		60
E 31	THE SKINNERS' COMPANY LADY NEVILLE CHARITY		UK	Very small	Yes	Yes	Yes		61
E 32	THE BERNARD SUNLEY CHARITABLE FOUNDATION		UK	Very large	Yes	Yes	Yes		61
E 33	ULSTER GARDEN VILLAGES Ltd.		Northern Ireland	Small	Yes	Yes	Yes		62
E 34	THE PRINCE OF WALES'S CHARITABLE FOUNDATION		UK	Medium	Yes	Yes	Yes		62
E 35	GARFIELD WESTON FOUNDATION		UK	Very large	Yes	Yes	Yes		63
E 36	THE WOLFSON FOUNDATION		UK	Very large	Yes	Yes	Yes		63
E 37	THE WOODROFFE BENTON FOUNDATION		UK	Large	Yes	Yes	Yes		64
E 38	WORLD MONUMENT FUND	World Monuments Watch	Worldwide	Large					64
F 1	THE ECOLOGY BUILDING SOCIETY	Ecology Mortgages	UK	Very large		Yes			66
F 2	TRIODOS BANK	Mortgages and loans	UK	Very large		Yes			67

Section A
STATUTORY SOURCES

Landfill Tax Credit Scheme

Nature of Funding	In 1996 the Government introduced a new tax on the disposal of waste in landfill sites. Built into it was a scheme whereby operators of landfill sites could claim tax credit for contributions made to approved environmental bodies. This is an entirely voluntary scheme.
Geographical Area	UK.
Eligible Applicants	Environmental bodies (EBs) enrolled with ENTRUST, the regulator of the landfill tax credit scheme. EBs must be non-profit distributing and not controlled by a landfill operator or local authority. Their constitution must allow support for at least one of the objects on the Customs and Excise list, which includes the maintenance, repair or restoration of a building or other structure which is a place of religious worship or of historic interest and the provision of financial, administrative and other services to enrolled environmental bodies. There is a non-refundable enrolling fee of £100. Organisations can enrol as umbrella EBs, enabling member groups to participate as associate bodies for a fee of £20. Umbrella organisations in Northern Ireland include the Ulster Wildlife Trust, tel: 01396 830282: NI 2000, tel: 01232 403779: Bryson House, tel: 01232 325835 and Arena Network, tel: 01232 410410.
Eligible Projects	Projects must conform to one of the "objects" listed in "Eligible Applicants" and must usually be within a 10 mile radius of a licensed landfill site. Most projects have to have ENTRUST approval before money can be transferred. The landfill operator is likely to want details of the project before agreeing to contribute.
Eligible Expenditure	All project costs.
Restrictions	Projects must allow some degree of public access, must not be operated for profit and must not directly benefit any contributing landfill operator.
Amount	Up to 20% of the contributing landfill operator's landfill tax liability. However, the money varies widely from council to council.
Form of Payment	Agreed between the EB and the landfill operator. When the EB receives the contribution, ENTRUST will invoice it for administration expenses.
Size of Fund	Very large.
Application Form?	Yes, for enrolling and for project approval. Available from ENTRUST or its website (see below).
Guidance Notes?	Yes, with ENTRUST's information pack.
Timetable	Usually applications should be lodged with the appropriate umbrella organisation between October and January.
Contact	ENTRUST
Address	ENTRUST, Suite 2, 5th Floor, Acre House, Town Hall Square, Sale, Cheshire M33 7WZ
Telephone	0161 972 0044
Fax	0161 972 0055
e-mail	judithcharlton@entrust.org.uk
Source	"Landfill Tax Information Note 8/96" (HM Customs and Excise); "Frequently Asked Questions" (ENTRUST); ENTRUST website.
Notes	About £120m is available for environmental projects each year. In 1998, almost 80% of potential landfill tax credits were donated. A copy of the Landfill Tax Registry (showing all licensed landfill sites) is available free of charge from HM Customs and Excise (tel. 0645 128 484; fax 0645 129 595; website www.hmce@gov.uk). Local authorities are also a good source of information. There is a list of enrolled EBs and projects on ENTRUST's website (www.entrust.org.uk). Because the registration fee is non-refundable, smaller organisations or those with only one project in mind may wish to approach landfill operators about funding before applying to enrol.

Nature of Funding	Grants to tackle the heating and insulation problems of low income households.
Geographical Area	Northern Ireland.
Eligible Applicants	Owner occupiers or tenants are eligible for grant if they are in receipt of attendance allowance, income support, income based job seekers allowance, housing benefit, family credit, disability work allowance, industrial injuries, disablement benefit or aged over 60.
Eligible Projects	Heating and insulation problems.
Eligible Expenditure	Grants towards loft insulation, draught proofing and advice on saving energy.
Restrictions	No grant will be paid if materials are purchased before approval has been granted.
Amount	Grant for loft insulation payable at a rate of 100% up to £198.70. Grant for draught-proofing payable at a rate of 100% up to £128.50. Grant for loft insulation and draught-proofing payable at a rate of 100% up to £305.00. Grant for energy advice £10.
Form of Payment	The grant is paid to the company who does the work, unless you do the work yourself. If you choose to do the work yourself, you can apply for a grant to cover the cost of materials only. The work costs more than the maximum grant available you may have to pay the extra cost yourself. If so, do not pay any money until you are satisfied with the work.
Size of Fund	Medium.
Application Form?	Yes.
Guidance Notes?	#
Timetable	#
Contact	#
Address	EAGA, Freepost, BE2107 Dungannon, Co. Tyrone BT70 5BR
Telephone	0800 181667
Fax	01868 753975
e-mail	#
Source	#
Notes	#

Nature of Funding	Grants for exterior work which will conserve or enhance the architectural or historic character of towns and villages that are designated conservation areas, and preserve the individual building or group of buildings on which that character depends. This grant has been SUSPENDED INDEFINITELY.
Geographical Area	Northern Ireland.
Eligible Applicants	Owners of buildings within a designated Conservation Area.
Eligible Projects	External repair and enhancement to the original fabric of buildings.
Eligible Expenditure	Work to the visible exterior facade using appropriate materials and design.
Restrictions	Work must commence within 6 months of the letter of offer. The building must be maintained in a reasonable state of repair and adequately insured against fire. The agreed schedule of Conservation Grant requirements must be adhered to throughout the entire project.
Amount	20% of the cost of eligible work together with 75% of the cost of professional fees.
Form of Payment	Mostly on completion on receipt of final accounts and architect's certificates. Stage payments can be arranged on larger projects.
Size of Fund	DUE TO OVERSUBSCRIPTION, CONSERVATION AREA GRANTS HAVE BEEN SUSPENDED INDEFINITELY.
Application Form?	Yes.
Guidance Notes?	Design Guide for each designated Conservation Area.
Timetable	#
Contact	Local Divisional Planning Offices. See p72 for relevant addresses.
Address	#
Telephone	#
Fax	#
e-mail	#
Source	#
Notes	Although the C/A grant has been suspended, some Conservation Areas are in receipt of Heritage Lottery Funding through the Townscape Heritage Initiative (see C 11). There is some element of grant from the Planning Service in some circumstances. Individual Planning Offices should be contacted before applying for THI.

Historic Buildings Grant

Nature of Funding	Grants to assist the repair and restoration of certain eligible items which constitute the historic fabric of the building.
Geographical Area	Northern Ireland.
Eligible Applicants	Any owner of a grade A, B+ or B1 building.
Eligible Projects	In most cases only buildings which are legally protected as grade A, B+ or B1 by the Environment & Heritage Service. Historic building grant is available towards the repair and maintenance of certain eligible items which constitute the historic fabric of a building. In exceptional circumstances grant may be paid when the approved alterations replace previous inappropriate works. Listed building consent is required for any works that may effect the character of a listed building, and it is advised that advice be sought at an early stage.
Eligible Expenditure	Grants may be available for repairs to the historic fabric of a listed building, with the highest priority being given to essential structural repairs. If a professional consultant is employed by an owner, a grant of 75% may be given towards the cost of a reasonably incurred fee. For grant calculation purposes this will only relate to the amount of eligible work to the historic fabric in the scheme.
Restrictions	Generally new works are not grant aided even if carried out in a sympathetic manner. Grants are not available to Government or Public Bodies as owners of listed buildings.
Amount	Rate of grant for eligible work are currently under review, but at present the rates are as follows: Grade A: 35%, Grade B+: 20%, Grade B1: 20%, Grade B2: nil. For ecclesiastical buildings see D2. All thatched buildings are grant aided at 75% with other grant eligible works grant aided according to grade. Listed buildings in large commercial ownership in categories A, B+ & B1 qualify for grant at a rate of 5% subject to a limit of £5,000 in addition, a ceiling of £50,000 only will be paid in any financial year. Applicants in receipt of housing benefit, income support, or family credit for a period of 6 months or more may be considered for an enhanced level of grant.
Form of Payment	Grant is paid in arrears subject to the Environment & Heritage Service being satisfied that work has been carried out to the agreed required standard. Work must NOT commence until written approval has been received from the Environment & Heritage Service.
Size of Fund	#
Application Form?	Yes.
Guidance Notes?	Yes.
Timetable	Applications acknowledged within 5 working days. Written enquiries responded to within 15 working days.
Contact	Protecting Historic Buildings.
Address	The Environment & Heritage Service, Built Heritage, 5–33 Hill Street, Belfast BT1 2LA
Telephone	01232 235000
Fax	01232 543111
e-mail	#
Source	Environment & Heritage Service: Technical note 57.
Notes	The overall grants policy is currently under review.

Nature of Funding	Partnerships with landowners to ensure the best management of scheduled monuments.
Geographical Area	Northern Ireland.
Eligible Applicants	Owner occupiers of a scheduled historic monument.
Eligible Projects	Under the Historic Monuments and Archaeological Objects (NI) Order 1995, the Department of the Environment for Northern Ireland may assist owners in maintaining scheduled monuments in good condition.
Eligible Expenditure	Owners are not obliged to spend money on fencing or repairs, and scheduling does NOT create any right of public access. The owner, however, is legally responsible for a monument.
Restrictions	To carry out ANY works affecting the condition of a scheduled monument it is necessary to apply for Scheduled Monument Consent from the Environment and Heritage Service in advance. Activities requiring consent include flooding or tipping operations, planting, ploughing, altering or removing masonry and inserting drains or service trenches.
Amount	The terms of an agreement are negotiable and will be limited to a number of years. Payments will be related to the size of the scheduled area.
Form of Payment	Payments will be settled annually in arrears. Capital payment sums may also be paid on a one-off basis and chosen on priority for agreed, necessary repairs to scheduled monuments.
Size of Fund	Very small.
Application Form?	Yes.
Guidance Notes?	In preparation.
Timetable	#
Contact	The relevant Field Monument Warden
Address	The Environment & Heritage Service, 5–33 Hill Street, Belfast BT1 2LA
Telephone	028 9054 3025
Fax	028 9054 3111
e-mail	#
Source	Environment and Heritage Service: Scheduled Historic Monuments in Northern Ireland.
Notes	Carrying out prohibited work on a scheduled monument without consent is punishable by fines. Deliberately damaging or destroying a scheduled monument can carry more substantial fines. Permission must always be sought in advance.

Nature of Funding	The Urban Development Grant UDG is a discretionary grant administered by the Department of the Environment, with the objectives of encouraging economic and physical regeneration in Belfast and Londonderry and of promoting job creation, inward investment and environmental improvement by the development of vacant, derelict or underused land and buildings.
Geographical Area	In Londonderry, the city centre and Waterside Business District is targeted. In Belfast, priority is currently given to schemes within the Making Belfast Work areas.
Eligible Applicants	Private individuals and businesses.
Eligible Projects	The UDG scheme encompasses most types of commercial property development, including offices, retail, industrial, tourism, entertainment and social. Inner/middle city housing is an ongoing priority. Schemes can be speculative or for owner occupation and grant may be paid towards the cost of refurbishment or extension of existing buildings or the creation of new buildings.
Eligible Expenditure	For owner occupation projects eligible construction costs and professional fees will be considered. For speculative schemes the shortfall will be considered being the difference between the total development cost and the value of a project in completion.
Restrictions	A high percentage of resources will be devoted to projects that create a significant impact. Good quality projects requiring grant less than £100,000 will be considered in exceptional circumstances.
Amount	A range of support is available. The amount of grant offered is the minimum required to trigger the project. This will usually take the form of a cash grant. For speculative schemes in Belfast a shortfall up to 30% of total development costs increasing up to 50% for those properties in Making Belfast Work areas may apply, with 30% in Londonderry. Owner occupier grants may also be paid on up to 50% of eligible building costs for refurbishment schemes, and up to 30% for new build. In addition rental guarantees, professional fees or loan guarantees may be available.
Form of Payment	Cash grant.
Size of Fund	Large.
Application Form?	Yes.
Guidance Notes?	Yes.
Timetable	#
Contact	For the Londonderry office contact: Londonderry Development Office, Orchard House, 40 Foyle Street, Londonderry BT48 6AT tel: 01504 319900.
Address	For Belfast contact: Belfast Regeneration Office, 5th floor, Brookmount Buildings, 42 Fountain Street, Belfast BT1 5EE
Telephone	01232 251917
Fax	01232 251976
e-mail	george.wasson@doeni.gov.uk
Source	#
Notes	It will be necessary to demonstrate that the project would not go ahead without UDG. Grant cannot be substituted for other public money. Where a project is to receive other public money the UDG must achieve substantial identifiable additional benefits. Any grant received from other public sector agencies for the same work will be netted off the UDG offer.

Cavity Wall grant

Nature of Funding	Grants towards cavity wall insulation.
Geographical Area	Northern Ireland.
Eligible Applicants	Homeowners.
Eligible Projects	If your home was built after 1930, it is likely to be of cavity wall construction. Most types of homes can be insulated. Flats or maisonettes can only be done if the whole block is insulated at the same time.
Eligible Expenditure	Grant only paid to installers participating in the scheme.
Restrictions	No local authorities or housing associations may apply. Not available to properties using electricity as the primary source of heating.
Amount	#
Form of Payment	The grant will be deducted from the price by the installer.
Size of Fund	Medium.
Application Form?	Ring the local Energy Efficiency Advice Centre.
Guidance Notes?	Yes.
Timetable	#
Contact	Energy Efficiency Advice Centre
Address	1–11 May Street, Belfast BT1 4NA
Telephone	Freephone 0800 512012
Fax	01232 246133
e-mail	all@belfeac.demon.co.uk
Source	#
Notes	#

Energy Efficiency Advice Centre *A8*

Condensing boiler grant

Nature of Funding	Grants of £200 to upgrade domestic heating systems.
Geographical Area	UK.
Eligible Applicants	Homeowners.
Eligible Projects	£200 grant offered towards the purchase of a high efficiency condensing boiler.
Eligible Expenditure	#
Restrictions	Only boilers made by recommended manufacturers and installed by qualified installer.
Amount	£200.
Form of Payment	The completed application form, with proof of the purchase and installation of the boiler, should be sent to the address below and the cheque should be sent out within 3 weeks.
Size of Fund	Medium.
Application Form?	Yes. Available from your local Energy Efficiency Advice Centre.
Guidance Notes?	Yes.
Timetable	Cheques should be received three weeks after the application form was sent off.
Contact	Energy Efficiency Advice Centre
Address	1–11 May Street, Belfast BT1 4NA
Telephone	Freephone 0800 512012
Fax	01232 246133
e-mail	all@belfeac.demon.co.uk
Source	#
Notes	Up to £140 cashback is available to help owners upgrade heating controls.

Nature of Funding	The NHMF was established in 1980 as a successor to the National Land Fund. It will provide financial assistance towards the acquisition, preservation and maintenance of land, historic buildings, and works of art of outstanding national importance. In practices it has always operated as a fund of last resort.
Geographical Area	UK.
Eligible Applicants	Responsible non-profit making bodies are eligible, usually charities having conservation as one of their main activities, e.g. the National Trust, local civic/conservation trusts and Local Authorities.
Eligible Projects	Applications should only be made to the Fund as a last resort, after trying all other sources.
Eligible Expenditure	#
Restrictions	#
Amount	There is no fixed rate for grants, but sums involved are usually substantial. Funds usually need to be matched £ for £.
Form of Payment	#
Size of Fund	Medium.
Application Form?	The Heritage Lottery Fund Main Grants application form is to be used.
Guidance Notes?	#
Timetable	#
Contact	Information and Communications Team
Address	Heritage Lottery Fund, Glendinning House, 6 Murray Street, Belfast BT1 6DN
Telephone	01232 310120
Fax	01232 310121
e-mail	N/A
Source	Information for Applicants (Heritage Lottery Fund).
Notes	#

Home Improvement grants: Common Parts Grants

Nature of Funding	Grants to improve or repair the common parts (such as halls, landings and staircases) of buildings containing one or more flats.
Geographical Area	Northern Ireland.
Eligible Applicants	Landlords or private tenants who are responsible for repairs.
Eligible Projects	Improvements of common parts of buildings containing one or more flats.
Eligible Expenditure	Repairs to halls, stairs, landings etc.
Restrictions	Grant will not be payable in the following circumstances: if the property was built or converted less than 10 years prior to the date of application for grant; if the property is a second or holiday home; if the applicant is a Housing Executive tenant or a tenant of a registered Housing Association.
Amount	The amount of grant available will be calculated by the Executive and will depend on the approved cost of the works and the applicants ability to contribute to the cost. Up to a maximum of £20,000.
Form of Payment	Grants will only be paid upon satisfactory completion of works, either in full payment or by interim payments.
Size of Fund	Medium.
Application Form?	Yes. Ask for a Preliminary Enquiry Form.
Guidance Notes?	Yes.
Timetable	The speed at which the grant is processed will depend on the level of demand and the money available. Equally it will depend on the applicant submitting in time all necessary documentation to the Executive.
Contact	The local Housing Executive Grants Office, see the full page advertisement in The Phone Book Business and Services Section.
Address	Housing Executive, see The Phone Book.
Telephone	#
Fax	#
e-mail	#
Source	#
Notes	Housing Executive officers are willing to discuss and advise applicants at any stage of the process. No work should commence until formal written approval has been received.

Home Improvement grants: Disabled Facilities Grants

Nature of Funding	Grants to provide special facilities in a dwelling for a person with a disability.
Geographical Area	Northern Ireland.
Eligible Applicants	Owner occupiers, landlords and private tenants.
Eligible Projects	Grants to make a home suitable for a person with a disability, based on the recommendation of an Occupational Therapist employed by the Local Health Board/Trust.
Eligible Expenditure	Works must be necessary and appropriate as recommended by an Occupational Therapist. These may include the provision of easier internal access within the dwelling, provision of bathroom facilities, improving heating, adapting lighting controls, making the provision and cooking of food easier.
Restrictions	Grant will not be payable in the following circumstances: if the property is a second or holiday home; if the work is not necessary or appropriate; if the applicant is a Housing Executive tenant or a tenant of a registered Housing Association; the works must also be reasonable and practicable given the age and condition of the property.
Amount	The amount of grant available will be calculated by the Executive and will depend on the approved cost of the works and the applicants ability to contribute towards the cost. Normally up to a maximum of £20,000, although this amount can be exceeded at the discretion of the Executive.
Form of Payment	Grants will only be paid upon satisfactory completion of works, either in full payment or in interim payments.
Size of Fund	Medium.
Application Form?	Yes. Ask for a Preliminary Enquiry Form.
Guidance Notes?	Yes.
Timetable	The speed at which the grant is processed will depend on the level of demand and the money available. Equally it will depend on the applicant submitting in time all necessary documentation to the Executive.
Contact	The local Housing Executive Grants Office, see the full page advertisement in The Phone Book Business and Services Section.
Address	Housing Executive, see The Phone Book.
Telephone	#
Fax	#
e-mail	#
Source	#
Notes	Housing Executive officers are willing to discuss and advise applicants at any stage of the process. No work should commence until formal written approval has been received.

Nature of Funding	Grants to make a property suitable for multiple occupation. Essential improvements or repairs may be carried out.
Geographical Area	Northern Ireland.
Eligible Applicants	Owners (landlords). Not available to occupants.
Eligible Projects	Grants to make a property suitable for multiple occupation.
Eligible Expenditure	Examples of eligible improvements or repairs could include the provision of additional toilet and cooking facilities. Means of escape from fire and other fire precautions will need to be installed in most cases.
Restrictions	Grant will not be payable in the following circumstances: if the property was built or converted less than 10 years prior to the date of application for grant; if the property is a second or holiday home.
Amount	The amount of grant available will be calculated by the Executive and will depend on the approved cost of the works and the potential for increased rental income. A rent assessment will be carried out. Up to a maximum of £30,000.
Form of Payment	Grants will only be paid upon satisfactory completion of works, either in full payment or by interim payments.
Size of Fund	Medium.
Application Form?	Yes. Ask for a Preliminary Enquiry Form.
Guidance Notes?	Yes.
Timetable	The speed at which the grant is processed will depend on the level of demand and the money available. Equally it will depend on the applicant submitting in time all necessary documentation to the Executive.
Contact	The Housing Executive HMO Offices are based in Belfast and Coleraine, see the full page advertisement in The Phone Book.
Address	Housing Executive, see The Phone Book.
Telephone	#
Fax	#
e-mail	#
Source	#
Notes	Housing Executive officers are willing to discuss and advise applicants at any stage of the process. No work should commence until formal written approval has been received.

Nature of Funding	Group Repair is a scheme based grant subsidy for the external improvement of private sector terraced properties.
Geographical Area	Northern Ireland.
Eligible Applicants	Owner occupiers and landlords.
Eligible Projects	Terraced properties where an area based approach has been agreed.
Eligible Expenditure	Up to a maximum of £10,500 for two storey properties. Up to a maximum of £12,500 for two and half/three storey properties.
Restrictions	Where a terrace fails to meet the following criteria: 1. The terrace must have a 30 year life span. 2. There must be at least 25% of participants in receipt of income related benefits. 3. A minimum of 75% of the properties must be in external disrepair.
Amount	#
Form of Payment	The work is organised and supervised by the Executive. All works are carried out by a single contractor who will be paid by the Executive upon satisfactory completion of works.
Size of Fund	Medium.
Application Form?	Participants in Group Repair are notified by the Executive of the scheme proposals. All participants are consulted and agree content. Similar to other forms of grant aid, each participant may have to make a contribution to work costs based on their income. The maximum payment towards group repair is 5% of the total cost of works.
Guidance Notes?	Available at Grant Offices.
Timetable	It takes approximately 18 months to get a Group Repair Scheme on site. This covers all activities from identification, consultation through to tendering and the appointment of a contractor.
Contact	For further information contact the Area Action Team on Belfast 240588.
Address	Northern Ireland Housing Executive, The Housing Centre, 2 Adelaide Street, Belfast.
Telephone	01232 240588
Fax	#
e-mail	#
Source	#
Notes	Housing Executive officers are willing to discuss and advise applicants at any stage of the process. No work should commence until formal written approval has been received.

Home Improvement grants: Minor Works Assistance

Nature of Funding	Grants to carry out minor improvements/repairs or to provide for the adaptation work for a person with a disability.
Geographical Area	Northern Ireland.
Eligible Applicants	Owner occupiers and private tenants. Applicants must be in receipt of a means tested benefit and may need to be over 60 years of age.
Eligible Projects	There are five different grants to carry out small scale improvements or adaptations. Staying Put, Elderly Resident Adaptation, Patch and Mend, Disabled Adaptations Grant and Lead Pipe Replacement.
Eligible Expenditure	Staying Put: available to owners & tenants of 60 years or over, who are in receipt of an income related benefit. Works include repairs to gutters, windows, etc or adaptations (handrail, ramps). Elderly Resident Adaptation: available to assist with alterations to accommodate an elderly relative or friend to reside permanently in the house. Work can include fitting handrails etc. Patch and Mend: if the house is in an urban Renewal Area assistance may be sought to carry out basic wind and weather proofing works. Disabled Adaptations Grant: Work as recommended by an Occupational Therapist. Lead Pipe Replacement: Grant to replace lead supply pipe from water main to property.
Restrictions	Grant will not be payable in the following circumstances: if the property is a second or holiday home; if the applicant is a Housing Executive tenant or a tenant of a registered Housing Association.
Amount	Up to £1,080 at any one time. Maximum £3,240 over three years.
Form of Payment	Grants will only be paid upon satisfactory completion of works.
Size of Fund	Medium.
Application Form?	Yes. Ask for a Preliminary Enquiry Form.
Guidance Notes?	Yes.
Timetable	The speed at which the grant is processed will depend on the level of demand and the money available. Equally it will depend on the applicant submitting in time all necessary documentation to the Executive.
Contact	The local Housing Executive Grants Office, see the full page advertisement in The Phone Book Business and Services Section.
Address	Housing Executive, see The Phone Book.
Telephone	#
Fax	#
e-mail	#
Source	#
Notes	Housing Executive officers are willing to discuss and advise applicants at any stage of the process. No work should commence until formal written approval has been received.

Home Improvement grants: Renovation Grants

Nature of Funding	Grants to improve or repair unfit dwellings.
Geographical Area	Northern Ireland.
Eligible Applicants	Owner occupiers, landlords or private tenants (who are responsible for repairing their homes).
Eligible Projects	The improvement of unfit dwellings.
Eligible Expenditure	Typical works include the eradication of damp, roof replacement, of chimneys, gutters, plaster work etc. Serious defects may be put right e.g. If there is no inside toilet or the wiring is dangerous.
Restrictions	Grant will not be payable in the following circumstances: if the property was built or converted less than 10 years prior to the date of application for grant; if the property is a second or holiday home; if the applicant is a Housing Executive tenant or a tenant of a registered Housing Association.
Amount	The amount of grant available will be calculated by the Executive and will depend on the approved cost of the works and the applicants ability to contribute towards the cost which will be means tested. Up to a maximum of £25,000.
Form of Payment	Grants may be mandatory or discretionary. Even if the grant is mandatory, the Housing Executive must be satisfied that renovation is the most appropriate way of dealing with the property. If the grant is discretionary the Housing Executive can decide whether to award grant or not. Grants will only be paid upon satisfactory completion of works. However, if the cost is very great, discretionary interim grants may be applied for.
Size of Fund	Medium.
Application Form?	Yes. Ask for a Preliminary Enquiry Form.
Guidance Notes?	Yes.
Timetable	The speed at which the grant is processed will depend on the level of demand and the money available. Equally it will depend on the applicant submitting in time all necessary documentation to the Executive.
Contact	The local Housing Executive Grants Office, see the full page advertisement in The Phone Book Business and Services Section.
Address	Housing Executive, see The Phone Book.
Telephone	#
Fax	#
e-mail	#
Source	#
Notes	Housing Executive officers are willing to discuss and advise applicants at any stage of the process. No work should commence until formal written approval has been received.

Home Improvement grants: Repairs Grants

Nature of Funding	Grants are only for works required where a Certificate of Disrepair or Public Health Notice has been served by the Local District Council on a landlord, agent, owner occupier or certain tenants.
Geographical Area	Northern Ireland.
Eligible Applicants	Owner occupiers, landlords, agents and some private tenants.
Eligible Projects	Grants payable when the Environmental Health Officer from the Local District Council has served a Statutory Notice.
Eligible Expenditure	There are two forms of Statutory Notice: Public Health Notice, work can start immediately. A Certificate of Disrepair served on the landlord or a tenant with a repairing obligation. Work must NOT start until formal written approval has been granted.
Restrictions	Grant will not be payable in the following circumstances: if the property is a second or holiday home; if the applicant is a Housing Executive tenant or a tenant of a registered Housing Association.
Amount	For both type of statutory notice the amount of grant will be calculated by the Executive taking into account the approved cost of the works, the NAV and tenure of the property.
Form of Payment	Grants will only be paid when the requirements of the statutory notice have been met.
Size of Fund	Medium.
Application Form?	Submit the statutory notice to the local Grant Office.
Guidance Notes?	Yes.
Timetable	The speed at which the grant is processed will depend on the level of demand and the money available. Equally it will depend on the applicant submitting in time all necessary documentation to the Executive.
Contact	The local Housing Executive Grants Office, see the full page advertisement in The Phone Book Business and Services Section.
Address	Housing Executive, see The Phone Book.
Telephone	#
Fax	#
e-mail	#
Source	#
Notes	Housing Executive officers are willing to discuss and advise applicants at any stage of the process. No work should commence until formal written approval has been received.

Section B
EUROPEAN FUNDING

> **All the current European programmes will cease on 31st December 1999 and all the funds are already fully subscribed. Negotiations are currently taking place and it appears that the new funding programme will probably be in place in Spring 2000.**
>
> **It has been decided that Northern Ireland and the Highlands and Islands will lose their Objective 1 status.**

Between 1994–1999 Northern Ireland has been in receipt of substantial funding from Europe. The economic and social potential of the Province have been enhanced with funding from a variety of sources ranging from the main stream Structural Funds, which encompassed the Community Initiatives, and the Special Support and Reconciliation programme. The Province was confirmed Objective 1 status in 1989 in recognition of its special economic and social needs, which allowed it greater funding to redress problems of poor economic development.

Funding was distributed through many different central and local channels.

European Structural Funds

Northern Ireland has benefited from the Structural Funds since 1989. Between 1994–99 £956 million was allocated to support developments within the region.
The Funds comprised:

- *The European Regional Development Fund (ERDF)*
- *The European Social Fund*
- *The European Agricultural Guidance and Guarantee Fund*
- *Financial Instrument for Fisheries Guidance*

Many urban and rural areas and the historic buildings within them have benefited from the disbursement of the Structural Funds. The subprograms that were particularly beneficial were

1. Economic development
2. Tourism
3. Physical and social environment
7. Agriculture and rural development

Within these subprograms the Environmentally Sensitive Areas Scheme (ESA) provided enhancement grants to farmers to restore traditional agricultural buildings

The Community Initiatives

Between 1994–1999 13 European Community initiatives were instigated, 9 of which were in operation within Northern Ireland. The initiatives that were most of benefit to historic buildings within Northern Ireland were:

- Interreg 11
- Leader11
- Adapt
- Urban

> **The Council of Ministers have agreed to 4 community initiatives for 2000–2006 replacing the 13 previous ones. These will be:**
>
> **URBAN**   **urban regeneration**
>
> **INTERREG**   **cross border co-operation**
>
> **LEADER**   **rural regeneration**
>
> **EQUAL**   **addressing inequalities in the labour market**

For further information about future funding contact:

Department of Finance & Personnel
Rosepark House
Upper Newtownards Road
Belfast
Tel: 01232 520400

Special Support Programme for Peace and Reconciliation

The Special Support Programme for Peace and Reconciliation has run for 5 years from 1994–1999.

The Special Programme funds were an additional community initiative specifically for Northern Ireland and the Republic of Ireland with their central emphasis on reconciliation. The programme benefited all communities whilst concentrating on those areas and sections of the population suffering most acute deprivation. The programme was responsible for the refurbishment and regeneration of many buildings in rural areas, under the Rural Regeneration sub-programme. *All funds are currently allocated.*

The Urban Regeneration sub-programme continues to have a large impact on the regeneration of Belfast and Londonderry (see entry A8).

The International Fund for Ireland

Two funding strands of the International Fund for Ireland have been fully subscribed, that is the Tourism Programme and the Urban Development Programme. However, the Disadvantaged Areas Initiative comprising the Community Economic Regeneration Scheme (CERS) and the Community Regeneration & Improvement Special Programme (CRISP) have continued funding (see B3 p.24) through the Department of the Environment.

Culture 2000 (provisional title)

Nature of Funding	Culture 2000 will replace the EU's three cultural funding programmes (Raphael, Kaleidoscope and Ariane) with a single integrated programme. The specific measures within the programme have yet to be finalised and adopted by the European Commission. The draft proposal (which is subject to change) outlines three Actions under which projects can quality: Action 1: Integrated projects covered by structured, multiannual, transnational cultural co-operation agreements – this includes specific measures to support the cultural heritage. All projects must involve at least seven Member States. Action2: Major projects – this support is for emblematic projects, substantial in scale and in scope, i.e. the European City of Culture. Action 3: Specific projects that fulfil a number of criteria based on themes such as increasing access and participation, the use of new technologies, working with young people, and raising the profile of European culture outside the EU. At least four eligible countries should be involved in each such project.
Geographical Area	EU Member States, EEA/EFTA countries, some Central and Eastern European countries.
Eligible Applicants	Public or private sector bodies. The programme aims to encourage transnational collaboration and further EU integration. The number of partner countries involve din projects varies between Actions.
Eligible Projects	Applicants are advised to study the full criteria under each Action. All Actions are, however, still under discussion and therefore subject to change before the programme is finally adopted. Action 1 will include "supporting co-operation projects designed to preserve, share, promote and protect at a European level, the common cultural heritage of European importance". Under Action2: "Integrated projects covered by structured, multiannual co-operation agreements", priority will be given to cultural heritage of European importance.
Eligible Expenditure	To be confirmed.
Restrictions	To be confirmed.
Amount	Varies between Actions. As a rule, the minimum grant will be ECU 50,000 and the maximum approximately ECU 1 million. As the programme is still at proposal stage, these figures could change.
Form of Payment	To be confirmed.
Size of Fund	Very large.
Application Form?	Will be available once the programme has been formally adopted and a call for proposals has been issued. Application forms are usually published on-line and can be downloaded.
Guidance Notes?	Yes – within application form (see above).
Timetable	It is envisaged that the programme will be finalised and adopted before the end of 1999, and the first call for proposals made early in 2000. There is some possibility that elements of the programme may be piloted during 2000.
Contact	EUCLID – UK Contact Point.
Address	46–48 Mount Pleasant, Liverpool L3 5SD
Telephone	0151 709 2564
Fax	0151 709 8647
e-mail	euclid@cwcom.net
Source	The International Arts Bureau, drawing on information in various issues of *The International Arts Navigator.*
Notes	Eligibility: The EEA/EFTA countries were Norway, Lichtenstein and Iceland. Central and Eastern European countries are eligible where Co-operation Agreements have been signed. The International Arts Bureau runs a free enquiry service about EU and other international cultural funding programmes, contacts, networks and policies abroad. Telephone 0171 403 0777 (Fax 0171 403 2009) or e-mail: enquiry.iab@mcmail.com website: www.euclid.co.uk

European Regional Development Fund (ERDF)

Nature of Funding	The Fund aims to provide support for projects which contribute to the development of regions identified as being in greatest economic need. It promotes local initiatives for regional economic development. This includes built heritage projects that can contribute, through, for example, conversion to provide local employment, or restoration to increase local tourism.
Geographical Area	Northern Ireland.
Eligible Applicants	District councils and owners of listed buildings.
Eligible Projects	Projects must conserve and maintain the built heritage of Northern Ireland and enhance the tourism potential of the area.
Eligible Expenditure	#
Restrictions	The applicant must show that the project could not go ahead, or would be severely restricted without ERDF support.
Amount	Maximum of 50% for private investment and 75%of public investment of eligible costs.
Form of Payment	#
Size of Fund	Limited within the Northern Ireland Single (Objective 1) Programme 1994–1999.
Application Form?	Yes.
Guidance Notes?	#
Timetable	The timetable from application to decision is two to three months.
Contact	#
Address	Environment & Heritage Service, 5-33 Hill Street, Belfast BT1 2LA.
Telephone	01232 543004
Fax	01232 543001
e-mail	#
Source	#
Notes	The European Structural Funds are currently being reformed. There will be a Transitional Objective 1 Programme and a Special Programme for Northern Ireland. The details of the programme will not be approved by the European commission until mid 2000.

Disadvantaged Areas Initiative: CERS and CRISP

Nature of Funding	The Community Economic Regeneration Scheme (CERS) and the Community Regeneration and Improvement Special Programme (CRISP) were introduced in 1988 and 1990 as a funding partnership between the Department of the Environment and the International Fund for Ireland. They aim to assist communities in the regeneration of the most disadvantaged areas of Northern Ireland. CRISP is aimed at smaller towns and villages with a population of under 10,000 while CERS is aimed at wards in larger towns with populations in excess of 10,000.
Geographical Area	Designated settlements in Northern Ireland.
Eligible Applicants	Registered community groups with the aim of economic, physical and social regeneration of their local area.
Eligible Projects	CERS aims to encourage projects which stimulate economic activity, provide retail and industrial facilities, reduce unemployment and improve the environment. CRISP has several aims including the enhancement of public spaces and property in targeted areas.
Eligible Expenditure	1. Property related core projects: including the regeneration of a derelict town centre property for use as business units, tourist accommodation or retail units. 2. Environmental improvement: improvement of public open spaces. 3. Urban development programme: grants to the commercial sector for improvement of derelict property to bring it into economic use.
Restrictions	#
Amount	Capital grant for a CERS core project is up to 80%. Projects must be self sustaining. Grant for CRISP projects is up to 80%, with 100% grant for environmental improvements. CRISP also provides 30% grants for the refurbishment of unused and underused town centre commercial property.
Form of Payment	#
Size of Fund	Large.
Application Form?	The DOE and the IFI have dedicated local staff who respond to any community group for advice and will help them work up an application for funding.
Guidance Notes?	Yes.
Timetable	Applicants will receive an initial response within four weeks.
Contact	Department of the Environment.
Address	Regional Development Office, Londonderry House, Chichester Street, Belfast BT1 4JB
Telephone	01232 252703
Fax	#
e-mail	#
Source	#
Notes	#

Section C
PUBLIC SOURCES

Nature of Funding	The Architectural Heritage Fund (AHF), a national charity active since 1976, introduced its programme of feasibility study grants in 1990. The aim of the programme is to help new buildings preservation trusts (BPTs) embark with confidence on their first project and to encourage established BPTs to take on projects of more than usual complexity.
Geographical Area	UK.
Eligible Applicants	Buildings preservation trusts (charities whose main "object" is the preservation of historic buildings).
Eligible Projects	Feasibility studies of buildings that are listed and/or in a conservation area, whose repair for re-use would be likely to qualify for an AHF loan (Section C Number 2) and which the BPT intends to acquire should the study indicate that the project would be viable.
Eligible Expenditure	Professional fees and other costs involved in an options appraisal and initial viability assessment to establish whether it is worth investigating a potential project in greater detail.
Restrictions	The AHF does not contribute to the cost of scaled drawings, comprehensive surveys, detailed structural analyses or costed specifications at feasibility study stage. It may be willing in some circumstances to offer a grant for a study that is already under way, but will not consider applications for studies that have already been completed.
Amount	Up to 75% of the study cost, with a normal maximum grant of £5,000. In exceptional circumstances the AHF may be willing to offer up to £7,500, provided this is not more than 75% of the cost of the study.
Form of Payment	On completion, as soon as the AHF is satisfied with the feasibility study report and has received copies of invoices for the study.
Size of Fund	Small.
Application Form?	Yes.
Guidance Notes?	Yes.
Timetable	Applications are considered at quarterly meetings and must be submitted at least five weeks before the meeting at which the decision will be taken.
Contact	Projects team.
Address	The Architectural Heritage Fund, Clareville House, 26–27 Oxendon Street, London SW1Y 4EL
Telephone	0207 925 0199
Fax	0207 930 0295
e-mail	ahf@ahfund.org.uk
Source	"Feasibility Studies: A Guide for Buildings Preservation Trusts" (The Architectural Heritage Fund, April 1998).
Notes	The AHF published a revised application pack in April 1998. This contains extensive guidance about what an eligible feasibility study should cover and must be referred to when completing the application form.

Nature of Funding	The Architectural Heritage Fund (AHF), a national charity active since 1976, provides working capital in the form of short term, low interest loans to help buildings preservation trusts (BPTs) and other charities undertake projects involving the acquisition, repair and/or conversion of historic buildings.
Geographical Area	UK.
Eligible Applicants	Buildings preservation trusts (charities whose main "object" is the preservation of historic buildings) and other organisations with charitable status.
Eligible Projects	The project must involve a change in the ownership (normally through its acquisition by the borrower) and/or in the use of a building which is on a statutory list and/or in a conservation area.
Eligible Expenditure	Acquisition, repair, conservation, alteration and rehabilitation (e.g. installation of services, basic fittings, landscaping, etc).
Restrictions	Every borrower must offer adequate security in the form either of a first charge (mortgage) over a property of sufficient value to support the loan (see "Amount") or of a formal repayment guarantee from a bank, local authority or other corporate body acceptable to the AHF.
Amount	Up to 75% of the estimated gross cost of any qualifying preservation project undertaken by a BPT. Loans to other charities are restricted to a maximum of 50% of estimated gross cost. The maximum loan is currently £500,000 for a BPT project and £250,000 for a project undertaken by any other charity. If a first charge is to be provided as security, the amount of the loan will not exceed 70% of the estimated open market value of the property over which the charge is taken. The loan period is normally two years. In some circumstances it may be three years. Simple interest at 4% per annum is payable at the time the loan or any part of it is repaid, and may rise to 3% above base rate if the loan is not repaid within the agreed period.
Form of Payment	After an initial advance when the loan is contracted, a loan secured by a first charge is normally disbursed in installments against architect's certificates as they are issued. A loan secured by a repayment guarantee is normally disbursed in a single installment when contracted.
Size of Fund	Very large.
Application Form?	Yes.
Guidance Notes?	Yes.
Timetable	Applications are considered at quarterly meetings and should be submitted at least six weeks before the meeting at which the decision will be taken.
Contact	Projects team.
Address	The Architectural Heritage Fund, Clareville House, 26–27 Oxendon Street, London SW1Y 4EL
Telephone	0207 925 0199
Fax	0207 930 0295
e-mail	ahf@ahfund.org.uk
Source	"AHF Loans: Notes for Applicants" (The Architectural Heritage Fund).
Notes	The AHF may be willing to offer a refundable loan preparation grant of up to £15,000 to a BPT whose loan application is essentially complete but indicates one or two areas where further professional work is required. For further information, contact the AHF.

Nature of Funding	The Architectural Heritage Fund (AHF), a national charity active since 1976, introduced its programme of project administration grants in 1993. The aim of the programme is to help buildings preservation trusts (BPTs) meet non professional costs incurred when developing a project from completion of a feasibility study to the point where an AHF loan can be contracted.
Geographical Area	UK.
Eligible Applicants	Buildings preservation trusts (charities whose main "object" is the preservation of historic buildings).
Eligible Projects	The project must be deemed likely to meet the criteria for an AHF loan (Section C Number 2). In addition, the applicant BPT must: (a) have completed a feasibility study and submitted a report that accords with criteria published by the AHF; (b) have resolved to take the project forward; (c) be able to demonstrate that, in principle, there is no reason why capital funding applications for the project should not succeed; (d) not have any paid administrative support or uncommitted resources in excess of £5,000.
Eligible Expenditure	Payment of a project administrator and other administrative costs relevant to the project.
Restrictions	Project administration grants may not be used for professional fees. A BPT is only eligible for one grant under the scheme.
Amount	£4,000 per grant.
Form of Payment	Grants are disbursed in four installments at quarterly intervals.
Size of Fund	Very small.
Application Form?	Yes.
Guidance Notes?	Yes.
Timetable	None. Applications will be considered and the outcome notified within four weeks of receipt.
Contact	Projects team.
Address	The Architectural Heritage Fund, Clareville House, 26–27 Oxendon Street, London SW1Y 4EL
Telephone	0207 925 0199
Fax	0207 930 0295
e-mail	ahf@ahfund.org.uk
Source	"Project Administration Grants: Notes for Applicants" (The Architectural Heritage Fund).
Notes	The AHF introduced a modified version of its former project administration grants scheme with effect from April 1999.

Nature of Funding	National Lottery funds may be available to assist with the costs of undertaking feasibility studies and design competitions for arts buildings prior to submission of the full project application.
Geographical Area	Northern Ireland.
Eligible Applicants	Organisations whether amateur or professional may qualify for Lottery funding. Registered charities, commercial organisations, local authorities or educational establishments may apply as long as they can demonstrate that the project will be available for substantial public use.
Eligible Projects	Firm preference will be given to applicants seeking substantial capital funding if a feasibility study has been carried out first. Applications for funding a feasibility study will be assessed on: the equality of the brief; a realistic timetable for the feasibility study; the extent to which the proposed project appears to meet all other relevant criteria for Lottery funding detailed in the guidance notes.
Eligible Expenditure	#
Restrictions	No individuals, no revenue and no retrospective funding.
Amount	The percentage of grant available is 50%. For feasibility studies where consultant/researcher's fees are between £5,000 – £10,000 applicants are expected to invite at least 3 tenders. Where fees are over £10,000 the Arts Council requires that tenders are invited from at least 3 consultants / researchers.
Form of Payment	In installments.
Size of Fund	From the Capital budget – approximately £2 million per annum in total.
Application Form?	Applicants should ask for the Architectural Design Competitions/Feasibility Studies Application Form.
Guidance Notes?	Yes.
Timetable	Applications can be made at any time.
Contact	The Lottery Department
Address	Arts Council of Northern Ireland, MacNeice House, 77 Malone Road, Belfast BT9 6AQ
Telephone	01232 667000
Fax	01232 664766
e-mail	lottery@artscouncil-ni.org
Source	#
Notes	Support from Lottery Funds towards a feasibility study is NOT an indication that the proposed project will ultimately receive support from Lottery Funds for the full project.

Capital Programme

Nature of Funding	National Lottery Arts Capital Funding can be used to create new buildings as well as extending or improving existing ones to achieve the maximum benefit for the general public through support for arts projects.
Geographical Area	Northern Ireland.
Eligible Applicants	Organisations whether amateur or professional may qualify for Lottery funding. Registered charities, commercial organisations, local authorities or educational establishments may apply as long as they can demonstrate that the project will be available for substantial public use.
Eligible Projects	Funding may be available for the purchase of buildings, the extension or refurbishment of old buildings, new buildings and for disabled access to arts buildings (for feasibility studies and architectural design competitions see C4) Grants are also available for the purchase of equipment, musical instruments and vehicles, (including recording, office, sound and lighting equipment).
Eligible Expenditure	No individuals, no revenue funding and no retrospective funding.
Restrictions	#
Amount	£2,000 – £2,000,000. 25% – 50% matching funding is required.
Form of Payment	In installments.
Size of Fund	Very large. Approximately £2 million per annum.
Application Form?	Yes. Request 'Building Projects' or 'Equipment Purchase' application form.
Guidance Notes?	A new 3 stage procedure will be in place by December 1999. It will comprise feasibility / economic appraisal; development; construction. This procedure is intended to ensure that building projects are developed, designed and costed through all stages and will be based on one application point per year.
Timetable	The Lottery Department
Contact	Arts Council of Northern Ireland, MacNeice House, 77 Malone Road, Belfast BT9 6AQ
Address	01232 667000
Telephone	01232 664766
Fax	#
e-mail	lottery@artscouncil-ni.org
Source	#
Notes	In order to manage the transition between systems there will be a MORATORIUM ON NEW APPLICATIONS for capital projects.

Capital programme

Nature of Funding	The capital programme supports the provision of community based facilities accessible by the main sections of the community, which may be supported by District Councils or voluntary organisations.
Geographical Area	Northern Ireland.
Eligible Applicants	The following criteria apply: facilities must be available to the whole community; they must be managed on a cross community basis; they must deliver programmes which at all times are aimed at cross-community contact. Priority will be given to proposals in areas where there has been evidence of community conflict, particularly in small towns and villages rather than main district centres.
Eligible Projects	#
Eligible Expenditure	#
Restrictions	#
Amount	Full economic appraisals are required for all proposals costing over £100,000. It is intended that the scale of projects agreed will reflect the size of the community which it is intended to serve, but there will be an upper cost level for grant purposes of £250,000. Grant will be at the rate of 75% on an agreed budget.
Form of Payment	#
Size of Fund	Very Large.
Application Form?	#
Guidance Notes?	Yes.
Timetable	#
Contact	#
Address	Central Community Relations Unit (CCRU), 20–24 Donegall Street, Belfast BT1 2GP
Telephone	01232 544524
Fax	01232 544500
e-mail	#
Source	#
Notes	#

Design Advice

Nature of Funding	The aim of the service is to improve the environmental performance of the UK's building stock through a network of approved consultants offering free guidance on building projects.
Geographical Area	UK.
Eligible Applicants	Those that intend to undertake the proposed project.
Eligible Projects	Normally the building/group of buildings must have a minimum floor area of 500 square meters.
Eligible Expenditure	#
Restrictions	#
Amount	Eligible projects can receive a free one day consultation or subsidised consultation over a longer period.
Form of Payment	Client reimbursed after consultation has taken place.
Size of Fund	Medium.
Application Form?	Yes.
Guidance Notes?	Yes.
Timetable	Site meetings arranged to suit client.
Contact	Noel Burns
Address	Design Advice, Building Research Establishment, Garston, Watford WD2 7JR
Telephone	01923 664731
Fax	01923 664787
e-mail	DesignAdvice@bre.co.uk
Source	Design Advice (DETR).
Notes	There are a number of free publications covering energy efficiency. More details available from the service.

Main Grants Programme: Capital Funding

Nature of Funding	The Heritage Lottery Fund (HLF) is one of the 12 lottery distributors in the UK. The Application Pack explains the nature of its funding of historic buildings and sites and the new two stage application process, which is mandatory for capital projects costing over £500,000 and for those seeking development funding (Section C Number 9). The capital funding programme includes museums and galleries, historic building and sites, libraries and archives, local heritage initiative, industrial transport and maritime projects, urban parks and the Townscape Heritage Initiative (see separate entry C11).
Geographical Area	UK.
Eligible Applicants	Any organisation or individual may apply, but grants are not currently available for individual buildings in private or commercial ownership, except when part of a scheme put forward by public or not-for-profit organisations.
Eligible Projects	The Strategic Plan (May 1999) named the HLF's four main priorities: heritage conservation, national heritage, local heritage and heritage access and education. Projects to conserve and protect the heritage; stand-alone access and education projects. Applications are assessed against seven criteria: the importance of the project to the heritage; conservation benefits; access benefits; additional public benefits; quality of design of the project; financial need and viability; and the strengths of the applicant organisation. The demonstrable social and economic benefits to the community is an increasingly important factor. The HLF will also assess whether the building is at immediate risk of loss; the urgency of repairs; and whether the project could be divided into phases. Applications for grants not exceeding £100,000 are particularly welcome.
Eligible Expenditure	Grants towards the cost of structural repairs and other conservation work to historic fabric or interiors; conversion to give an historic building a viable long term use; acquisition for permanent preservation; archaeological investigation as a part of a project; improving access for all where compatible with the historic fabric; widening and enhancing study, understanding and enjoyment of the built heritage. Visitor facilities may be eligible in certain circumstances.
Restrictions	No assistance for routine maintenance, feasibility studies, furnishings or fittings. No retrospective funding. Complex projects costing over £500,000 are subject to a new two stage application process and may require a Conservation Plan. Projects costing under £5,000 are not normally considered.
Amount	When total eligible costs are less than £100,000, up to 90% funding; when costs are £100,000 or more, up to 75% funding. No upper limit. A proportion of partnership funding can be "in kind" support or voluntary labour. At least 5% (for projects up to £100,000) and 10% (for more costly projects) should be cash.
Form of Payment	Normally within 18 working days of receipt of invoices, at the percentage rate agreed for the total project cost.
Size of Fund	Very large.
Application Form?	Yes.
Guidance Notes?	Yes.
Timetable	The HLF aims to process single stage and stage one applications within six months. Success at stage one does not automatically mean an application will succeed at stage two.
Contact	Information and Communications Team
Address	Heritage Lottery Fund, Glendinning House, 6 Murray Street, Belfast BT1 6DN
Telephone	01232 310120
Fax	01232 310121
e-mail	#
Source	"Information for Applicants" (Heritage Lottery Fund).
Notes	The HLF has special provisions for buildings preservation trust projects. Contact Information and Communications Team.

Project Development Grants

Nature of Funding	The Heritage Lottery Fund (HLF) will consider contributing to the cost of developing a proposed capital project to the point where it is able to proceed to the second stage of an HLF Main Grants Programme application. Support is limited to specific technical and heritage elements.
Geographical Area	UK.
Eligible Applicants	As for Main Grants Programme (Section C Number 8).
Eligible Projects	Projects awarded a stage one pass in the Main Grants Programme (Section C Number 8) or Townscape Heritage Initiative (Section C Number 11).
Eligible Expenditure	Specific technical and heritage elements such as the preparation of detailed designs, the cost of employing quantity surveyors and other professionals, and specialist conservation studies such as the preparation of conservation and restoration plans.
Restrictions	No assistance with the preparation of options appraisals, preparation of business plans, market research, market analysis or other business-related studies.
Amount	Up to 75% of total eligible costs, with no upper limit on amount.
Form of Payment	Normally within 18 working days of receipt of invoices, at the percentage rate agreed for the total project cost.
Size of Fund	Very large.
Application Form?	Yes.
Guidance Notes?	Yes.
Timetable	#
Contact	The HLF aims to process applications within six months. Information and Communications Team.
Address	Heritage Lottery Fund, Glendinning House, 6 Murray Street, Belfast BT1 6DN
Telephone	01232 310120
Fax	01232 310121
e-mail	#
Source	"Information for Applicants" (Heritage Lottery Fund).
Notes	#

Revenue Grants Programme

Nature of Funding	In 1998 the HLF introduced a programme specifically to support revenue funded projects. The grant aims to widen and enhance popular access to the heritage.
Geographical Area	UK.
Eligible Applicants	Any organisation or individual may apply.
Eligible Projects	The four aims of the grant scheme are: developing new audiences for the heritage; delivering educational benefits particularly to children and young people; increasing study, understanding and enjoyment of the heritage; and encouraging active participation by all in heritage activities.
Eligible Expenditure	The grant scheme will support self contained, fixed term projects, normally for up to three years, which offer sustainable benefits that will continue beyond the period of lottery funding.
Restrictions	The HLF will not fund core staff and running costs or retrospective applications.
Amount	Up to £100,000 for a three year period. The applicant organisation should be able to fund 10% of the cost. No more than 20% of the project cost should be for administration and overheads. Up to 25% of the project costs may relate to capital equipment.
Form of Payment	90% of the grant is payable in quarterly payments in advance, on receipt of the appropriate invoice. 10% of the grant is retained until completion of the project.
Size of Fund	Very large.
Application Form?	Yes.
Guidance Notes?	Yes.
Timetable	The HLF aims to provide a decision within 6 months.
Contact	Information and Communications Team.
Address	Heritage Lottery Fund, Glendinning House, 6 Murray Street, Belfast BT1 6DN
Telephone	01232 310120
Fax	01232 310121
e-mail	#
Source	"Information for Applicants" (Heritage Lottery Fund).
Notes	Although this fund does NOT cover capital costs for building restoration, it can provide for the interpretation of the monument or building, increase public awareness in the built heritage.

Nature of Funding	The Townscape Heritage Initiative (THI) was launched in April 1998 to support strategic action to address problems of disrepair, erosion of quality and under use of buildings in designated conservation areas. The programme will run for at least three years.
Geographical Area	UK.
Eligible Applicants	Single organisations such as local authorities, partnerships and less formally structured consortia. The local authority will be expected to demonstrate its commitment by membership of the partnership.
Eligible Projects	THI will give priority to schemes in areas of social and economic deprivation. Proposed schemes should be large enough to have an impact on the historic area as a whole and may include the repair of the structure and external envelope of historic buildings and structures; authentic reinstatement of architectural features of historic buildings and their settings; bringing vacant floor space in historic buildings back into use; filling gap sites in established frontages with appropriate, buildings; repair and authentic reinstatement of elements lost from urban green spaces, historic surfaces and other "public realm" townscape features. Bids will be judged on the heritage merit of the proposed schemes; the conservation and public benefits; the need for public sector investment to solve major problems; technical quality; financial viability; and organisational strength.
Eligible Expenditure	The partners contribute to a common fund to which the Heritage Lottery Fund (HLF) also contributes. The common fund can be used to meet the cost of a project officer or team and to make grants towards the cost of eligible work undertaken by property owners and work to the public realm (see above). The power to make offers will normally be delegated to the partnership and monitored on behalf of the HLF. Where necessary, grants of up to 50% of the cost of developing a full Stage 2 application will be available to successful Stage 1 applicants.
Restrictions	Major projects only. THI does not apply to single buildings or groups of buildings in single ownership. Buildings in areas covered by a THI may not normally apply to the Main Grants Programme (Section C Number 8).
Amount	20% to 50% of costs – in exceptional cases 75%.
Form of Payment	By installment on evidence of expenditure.
Size of Fund	Very large.
Application Form?	Yes.
Guidance Notes?	Yes.
Timetable	Stage 1 applications in the second (of three) THI rounds were due by 21 May 1999 with "in principle" indications from the HLF in late September. Stage 2 applications are then due by mid February 2000 with decisions announced by the HLF in April 2000. The timetable for the third round has not yet been announced.
Contact	Information and Communications Team.
Address	Heritage Lottery Fund, Glendinning House, 6 Murray Street, Belfast BT1 6DN
Telephone	01232 310120
Fax	01232 310121
e-mail	#
Source	"The Townscape Heritage Initiative" (Heritage Lottery Fund).
Notes	There are 53 designated Conservation areas in Northern Ireland. In the 1998 and 1999 bidding rounds over £8 million grant was awarded to projects within 13 conservation areas. This funding will be of major benefit to both the historic buildings and the economy of some of Northern Ireland's most historic towns and villages.

Small grants for small groups

Nature of Funding	Small grants (between £500 – £5,000) to help meet the needs of those at greatest disadvantage in society, and to improve the quality of life in the community.
Geographical Area	UK.
Eligible Applicants	A group set up for charitable purposes (not necessarily a registered charity) whose gross income last year was under £15,000.
Eligible Projects	Although the main thrust of the funding is towards social benefit, repairs and improvements to premises owned or leased by the group can be grant aided.
Eligible Expenditure	If grant is paid towards building repair, the group must own or lease the building. There is also a minimum tenancy depending on the size of grant. If planning permission is required it must be applied before applying for grant.
Restrictions	No grants to individuals, profit-making companies, local or health authorities. No NHS trusts,, schools, appeals supporting statutory bodies. No grants for endowments, loan payments, no retrospective funding. It is UNLIKELY that funds will be allocated to projects more properly the responsibility of the Sports Council, Arts Council or Heritage Lottery Fund.
Amount	Between £500 – £5,000.
Form of Payment	If successful the applicants will receive the grant one month after acceptance. The grant must be spent within 6 months.
Size of Fund	Medium.
Application Form?	Yes.
Guidance Notes?	Yes.
Timetable	Applicants will receive a cheque one month after being notified of their successful application.
Contact	Small Grants Team.
Address	National Lottery Charities Board, 2nd Floor, Hilden House, 30–34 Hill Street, Belfast BT1 2LB
Telephone	01232 551455
Fax	01232 551431
e-mail	#
Source	The application pack is also available on the Internet www.nclb.org.uk
Notes	#

Nature of Funding	The New Opportunities Fund will support the creation of new healthy living centres and the expansion and enhancement of existing ones. Both revenue & capital projects will be funded but only limited funds will be available for buildings.
Geographical Area	UK.
Eligible Applicants	Awards will be made to partnerships or organisations. These may include: local authorities, Health & Social Services Boards, local health service organisations, voluntary and community groups, private sector organisations, local health groups.
Eligible Projects	Projects that promote health in its broadest sense such as 'green gyms', credit unions, food co-ops. Such projects may include the major refurbishment of an existing building. For any building project over £250,000 a registered architect must be employed at the development phase.
Eligible Expenditure	#
Restrictions	No retrospective grants. No funding for projects that promote specific religious beliefs. Funding will not replace statutory support. Grant will be unlikely to partners whose main business or activities are contrary to healthy living (e.g. tobacco companies).
Amount	There is no fixed limit. Awards over £1 million will be unlikely. If you are applying for grant of over £250,000 you will be expected to produce substantial supporting documentation at the second application stage. 100% grant will not be paid.
Form of Payment	During the life of the grant you will be expected to raise funds from other sources and develop a broad continuous funding base.
Size of Fund	Very large. £300 million has been allocated over the next 3 years.
Application Form?	Yes. There is a two stage application process.
Guidance Notes?	Yes.
Timetable	#
Contact	#
Address	New Opportunities Fund, PO Box 1220, Belfast BT7 2AL
Telephone	0845 6004848
Fax	#
e-mail	#
Source	#
Notes	The New Opportunities Fund is the sixth 'Good Cause' supported by the National Lottery. Other grant programmes include 'Out of School Activities'; ICT training for teachers and school librarians; cancer prevention treatment, detection and care; green spaces and sustainable communities and community access to lifelong learning.

Tourism Development Scheme

Nature of Funding	The Tourism Development Scheme will consider grant aiding the provision of self catering units on condition that they are sustainable environmentally, socially and economically, will add to Northern Ireland's tourist industry, will create additional employment, will be of a high standard and would not go ahead without assistance.
Geographical Area	Northern Ireland.
Eligible Applicants	Public, private and voluntary sector projects may be eligible.
Eligible Projects	Priority for financial assistance will be for: the conversion of existing rural (including village) properties resulting in no less than 2 lettable units. Such development must largely maintain the appearance and size of the existing building and are required to match the standards of Rural Cottage Holidays Ltd (a previous NITB initiative). New build development of at least 6 units in key tourist areas (holiday village) will also be funded.
Eligible Expenditure	#
Restrictions	#
Amount	The is no fixed level of assistance. It will be the minimum needed in each case to allow the project to proceed. The Board contributes on average 25%–30% of the project costs.
Form of Payment	#
Size of Fund	Large.
Application Form?	#
Guidance Notes?	#
Timetable	#
Contact	Northern Ireland Tourist Board
Address	Investment Division, St Anne's Court, 59 North Street, Belfast BT1 1NB
Telephone	01232 231221
Fax	01232 240960
e-mail	#
Source	#
Notes	Until 1999 the NITB administered 3 sources of funding: their own Tourism Development Scheme; the European Union funded programmes and the International Fund for Ireland. These latter two programmes are fully subscribed and cease in December 1999. They were crucial in the development of tourist facilities in rural areas. It is not known what European funding will be made available for the development of Tourism in 2000.

Nature of Funding	The Lottery Sports Fund distributes funds to a Capital Programme; the Development of Talented Individuals Programme and the Major International Events Programme.
Geographical Area	Northern Ireland.
Eligible Applicants	Voluntary organisations, charity; community groups; local authorities and other public sector establishments including educational establishments; and private companies (provided that the project is not for private gain). Projects must normally have a value of £5,000 or more.
Eligible Projects	Support towards the provision of sports facilities and equipment. This will only be relevant where the facilities are housed in, or within the curtilage of, an historic building.
Eligible Expenditure	#
Restrictions	The capital programme is currently under review with no new applications being sought.
Amount	Previous applications were funded up to a maximum of 70% depending on the project. Funding amounts are currently under review.
Form of Payment	#
Size of Fund	Large.
Application Form?	Yes. A two stage application was in operation. Contact the Lottery Sports Fund for current information.
Guidance Notes?	Yes.
Timetable	Applications were judged on a rolling programme and took up to 3 months to assess. A new timetable may be introduced in 2000.
Contact	The Lottery Sports Fund
Address	Sports Council for Northern Ireland, House of Sport, Upper Malone Road, Belfast BT9 5LA
Telephone	01232 382222
Fax	01232 383822
e-mail	#
Source	#
Notes	The capital programme is currently under review and the new programme will be launched in 2000.

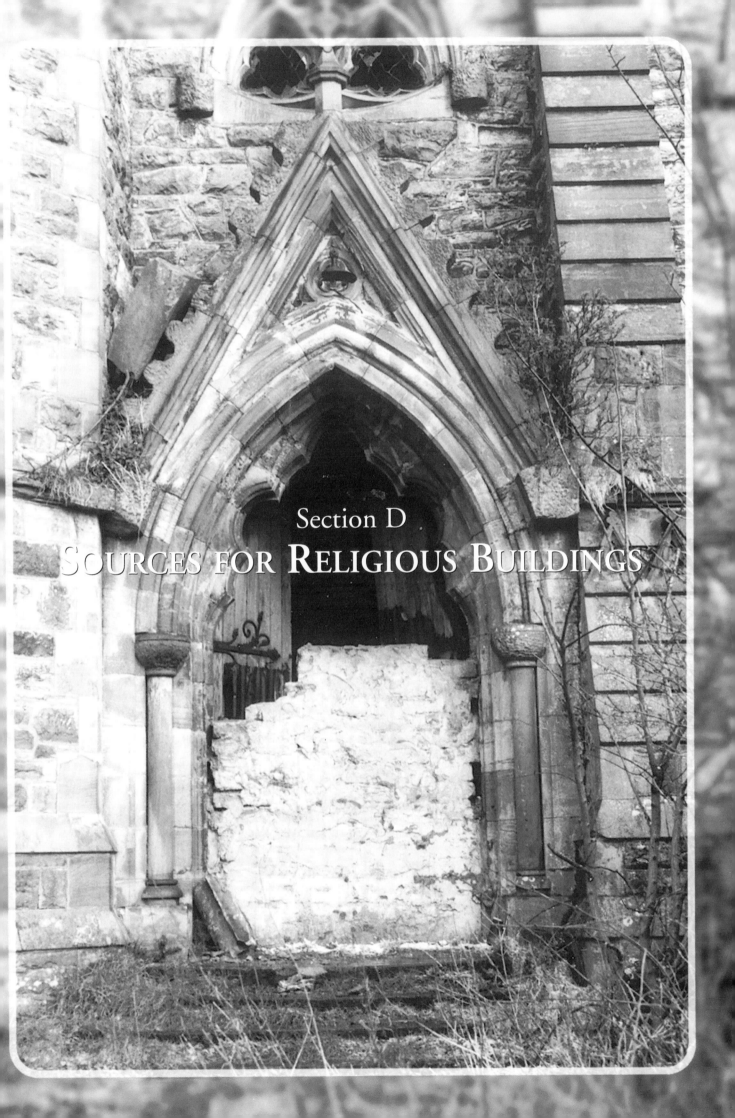

Section D
SOURCES FOR RELIGIOUS BUILDINGS

Unlike England, where the Council for the Care of Churches has some grants available for the conservation of church furnishings and fittings, the care of ecclesiastical buildings that are still in use is largely the responsibility of the immediate parish. In most denominations there is recourse to the higher church body, be it diocese or representative council but there is no guarantee of funding for the restoration of the fabric of the building.

The Environment & Heritage Service have an enhanced rate of grant of $33^{1}/3\%$ for Grade A & B+ buildings (see D2). The Heritage Lottery Fund will also grant aid church restoration. Several of the Trusts featured in Section E will fund the restoration of ecclesiastical buildings, (see Quick Reference Guide for details).

Possible sources of advice:

Roman Catholic Church

Archdiocese of Armagh
Diocesan Secretary
Ara Coeli
Armagh
Tel: 01861 522045

Church of Ireland

The Secretary
Representative Church Body
Church of Ireland House
Church Avenue
Rathmines
Dublin 6
Tel: 003531 4978422

Presbyterian Church

The Presbyterian Church in Ireland
Church House
Fisherwick Place
Belfast BT1 6DW
Tel: 01232 322284

Methodist Church

Methodist Church in Ireland
The Property Board
1 Fountainville Avenue
Belfast BT9 6AN
01232 324554
01960 322270

Interchurch Reconciliation Fund for Ireland
NB This has no fund for the building repairs

Tel: 01232 663145

Ulster Historic Churches Trust
NB This has no fund for the building repairs

Hon Secretary
Rev. Trevor Williamson
012477 38368

Historic Buildings Grant

Nature of Funding	Grants to assist the repair and restoration of the best of Northern Ireland's ecclesiastical buildings.
Geographical Area	Northern Ireland
Eligible Applicants	Churches of all denominations or religions in use for public worship, through the body responsible for the maintenance of the building.
Eligible Projects	Churches or their churchyards must be of Grade A or B+ to be eligible for funding.
Eligible Expenditure	Grant may be available towards repair and restoration of eligible items which constitute the historic fabric of the building. If a professional consultant is employed by an owner, a grant of 75% may be given towards the cost of a reasonably-incurred fee. For grant calculation purposes, this will only relate to the amount of eligible work to the historic fabric in the scheme.
Restrictions	Generally, new works are not grant-aided even if carried out in a sympathetic character. However, grant may be paid in exceptional circumstances when the approved alterations replace previous inappropriate works.
Amount	Grade A and B+ ecclesiastical buildings can receive $33^1/3\%$ grant for eligible works. There is no grant available for lower grades.
Form of Payment	Grant is paid in arrears subject to Environment & Heritage Service being satisfied that work has been carried out to the agreed required standard. Work must not commence without prior written approval from Environment & Heritage Service.
Size of Fund	#
Application Form?	Yes.
Guidance Notes?	Yes.
Timetable	Applications acknowledged within 5 working days. Written enquiries responded to within 15 working days.
Contact	Protecting Historic Buildings.
Address	The Environment & Heritage Service, Built Heritage, 5–33 Hill Street, Belfast BT1 2LA
Telephone	01232 235000
Fax	01232 543111
e-mail	N/A
Source	Environment & Heritage Service: Technical Note 57
Notes	The overall grants' policy is currently under review.

Nature of Funding	The Irish Ecumenical Church Loan Fund gives low interest loans to a variety of church and community projects. The Fund will provide loans for the purchase or refurbishment of buildings.
Geographical Area	Ireland
Eligible Applicants	Loans only made to groups and organisations.
Eligible Projects	#
Eligible Expenditure	#
Restrictions	No individuals.
Amount	Loans will not normally exceed £15,000 (the maximum possible loan is £25,000), to be repaid within 7 years.
Form of Payment	#
Size of Fund	Small
Application Form?	On the application form available from ECLOF.
Guidance Notes?	Yes.
Timetable	The Committee meets in March and September. Applications to be sent in a month in advance.
Contact	#
Address	Irish Ecumenical Church Loan Fund, Inter-Church Centre, 48 Elmwood Avenue, Belfast BT9 6AZ
Telephone	01232 663145
Fax	01232 381737
e-mail	#
Source	#
Notes	The Secretary of the Fund is available in the office on Wednesday mornings for consultation by telephone or in person.

Section E
CHARITABLE TRUSTS

All Churches Trust Limited *E1*

Nature of Funding	Grants in support of churches and charities preserving UK heritage. All applications are considered on their merits within the broad guidelines outlined below. Grants are made out of income derived from the Ecclesiastical Insurance Office plc.
Geographical Area	UK.
Eligible Applicants	Organisations with charitable status and religious establishments only.
Restrictions	No national charities or those with political associations. No individuals.
Amount	£100 – £5,000.
Form of Payment	Usually one-off.
Size of Fund	Small.
Application Form?	Application form available from the Trust.
Guidance Notes?	Yes.
Timetable	All applications are acknowledged after the Trustees' decision.
Contact	The Company Secretary
Address	Allchurches Trust Limited, Beaufort House, Brunswick Road, Gloucester GL1 1JZ
Telephone / Fax / e-mail	01452 528533
Source	"Statement of Policy and Guidelines for Applicants" Allchurches Trust.
Notes	#

Lord Barnby's Foundation *E2*

Nature of Funding	The Foundation will consider giving grants for the preservation of buildings, both religious and secular, of historic or architectural interest.
Geographical Area	UK.
Eligible Applicants	Organisations with charitable status and religious establishments only.
Restrictions	No financial assistance for individuals. In the case of religious buildings, only cathedrals or buildings of comparable scale are considered.
Amount	£1,000 – £5,000.
Form of Payment	#
Size of Fund	Large.
Application Form?	By letter, describing the applicant organisation and the project. A copy of the previous year's audited accounts should be enclosed.
Guidance Notes?	No.
Timetable	Trustees meet three times a year. Applications can be submitted at any time.
Contact	John Billing
Address	Lord Barnby's Foundation, Messrs Payne Hicks Beach, 10 New Square, Lincoln's Inn, London WC2A 3QG
Telephone / Fax / e-mail	0171 465 4300
Source	#
Notes	#

Nature of Funding	The Foundation has in the past offered grants for the preservation of religious buildings of historic or architectural interest.
Geographical Area	UK.
Eligible Applicants	Registered charities only.
Restrictions	No individuals.
Amount	There is no limit.
Form of Payment	#
Size of Fund	Large, but see Notes below.
Application Form?	Applicants should write describing their organisation, the project and the need for the grant.
Guidance Notes?	No.
Timetable	Trustees meet to consider applications in April and November.
Contact	Miss J Ford, Administrator
Address	The Beaverbrook Foundation, 11 Old Queen Street, London SW1H 9JA
Telephone / Fax / e-mail	0171 222 7474 / 0171 222 2198
Source	#
Notes	The Foundation's funds are fully committed, and it is therefore unable to accept applications for the time being.

William Adlington Cadbury Charitable Trust   *E4*

Nature of Funding	Grants are available for the preservation of listed buildings and monuments.
Geographical Area	UK, but especially the West Midlands.
Eligible Applicants	Organisations with charitable status only.
Restrictions	No individuals.
Amount	£100 – £5,000.
Form of Payment	Usually one-off.
Size of Fund	Small.
Application Form?	There is no application form. Apply by letter, giving the applicant's charity registration number, a brief description of its activities, details of the specific project for which the grant is requested, a budget for the proposed work and details of funds already raised for the project. Enclose a copy of the organisation's most recent accounts.
Guidance Notes?	Yes.
Timetable	Trustees meet twice yearly. Applications will not be acknowledged unless a stamped addressed envelope is enclosed.
Contact	The Secretary
Address	William Adlington Cadbury Charitable Trust, 2 College Walk, Selly Oak, Birmingham B29 6LQ
Telephone / Fax / e-mail	0121 472 1464
Source	#
Notes	#

Investors in Society

Nature of Funding	Investors in Society provides loans for short-term working capital needs; bridging loans, property development etc.
Geographical Area	UK and Ireland.
Eligible Applicants	Charities, Churches, voluntary and community groups, unincorporated associations and social enterprises for charitable purposes.
Restrictions	Loans will not be commuted to grants.
Amount	£5,000 – £100,000.
Form of Payment	#
Size of Fund	Large.
Application Form?	Application form available from the Charities Aid Foundation. Include information about the organisation including audited accounts.
Guidance Notes?	Yes.
Timetable	Applications can be made at any time.
Contact	Michael J. Hicks, Loan Fund Manager
Address	CAF Community Finance, 25 King's Hill Avenue, West Malling, Kent ME19 4TA
Telephone / Fax / e-mail	01732 520029 / 01732 520123 / iis@caf.charitynet.org
Source	#
Notes	Discussion by telephone about a project is welcomed.

The Chase Charity E6

Nature of Funding	The Trustees will consider giving grants for the preservation of parish churches, almshouses and some other small buildings, usually in rural areas, in community use and of architectural merit.
Geographical Area	UK (except Greater London).
Eligible Applicants	Organisations with charitable status or exempt charitable status only.
Restrictions	No individuals. No support for large organisations or their branches, large or widely circulated appeals, or any body applying to the Millennium Lottery Board.
Amount	£1,000 – £10,000.
Form of Payment	#
Size of Fund	Large.
Application Form?	By letter describing the applicant, the project and its timescale, the financial need and other sources of assistance. Enclose annual report and accounts. All applicants receive a response except circular appeals.
Guidance Notes?	Yes.
Timetable	The Trustees meet quarterly, but because there is a waiting list, applications are rarely considered within three months of receipt. The applicant may be asked for further information and advised when to write back. Staff try to visit every project which may be considered by the Trustees.
Contact	Miss A Hornsby
Address	The Chase Charity, 2 The Court, High Street, Harwell, Didcot, Oxfordshire OX11 0EY
Telephone / Fax / e-mail	01235 820044
Source	#
Notes	#

Nature of Funding	Under its Heritage and Arts category of charitable-giving, the Foundation offers grants for the preservation of secular buildings of historic or architectural interest.
Geographical Area	UK.
Eligible Applicants	Organisations with charitable status only.
Restrictions	No individuals. No support for schools or colleges unless they have a long-standing connection with the Clothworkers' Company. No grant towards the maintenance or restoration of ecclesiastical buildings unless they have a long-standing connection with the Clothworkers' Company, or unless they are appealing for a specific purpose which is considered to be of outstanding importance to the national heritage.
Amount	£1,000 – £50,000.
Form of Payment	One-off.
Size of Fund	Very large, but see Notes below.
Application Form?	By letter (preferably not more than 2.5 sides of A4) on the applicant charity's official notepaper. Enclose annual report, audited accounts, outline of project and costing, and completed "data information sheet" (available from the Foundation).
Guidance Notes?	Yes.
Timetable	The Trusts and Grants committee meet six times a year, and there is a rolling programme of processing applications. A decision may take up to 12 weeks. All applications are acknowledged, and both successful and unsuccessful applicants are notified by letter.
Contact	Mr M G T Harris
Address	The Clothworkers' Foundation, Clothworkers' Hall, Dunster Court, Mincing Lane, London EC3R 7AH
Telephone / Fax / e-mail	0171 623 7041
Source	#
Notes	Grants in the Foundation's Heritage and Arts category amounted to £156,000 in 1998.

The John S Cohen Foundation   E8

Nature of Funding	The Foundation will consider making grants for the preservation of secular buildings, preferably linked to education or training, but the programme is very limited.
Geographical Area	UK.
Eligible Applicants	Organisations with charitable status only.
Restrictions	No individuals.
Amount	Limited.
Form of Payment	#
Size of Fund	Large.
Application Form?	By letter, outlining the project and the applicant's activities and finances.
Guidance Notes?	No.
Timetable	Meetings are normally every March and October and applications must arrive one month before the meeting. Only successful applicants receive a response.
Contact	The Administrator
Address	The John S Cohen Foundation, 85 Albany Street, London NW1 4BT
Telephone / Fax / e-mail	0171 486 1117 / 0171 486 1118
Source	#
Notes	#

Nature of Funding	Priorities of the Fund may vary from year to year. The Trustees consider applications for projects assisting cross-community groups, self help, assistance to the unemployed and groups helping the disadvantaged.
Geographical Area	Northern Ireland.
Eligible Applicants	Organisations with charitable status.
Restrictions	No individuals. Normally grants are not made to playgroups or sporting groups outside the Antrim Borough.
Amount	Up to £6,000. Average grant size £500.
Form of Payment	#
Size of Fund	Very small.
Application Form?	By letter, including details of the applicant and their charitable status. Enclose annual report, audited accounts, outline of project and costings.
Guidance Notes?	Yes.
Timetable	All applications must be accompanied by a stamped, addressed envelope. Trustees meet quarterly. All applicants will be advised of the Trustees' decision.
Contact	The Secretary
Address	Enkalon Foundation, 25 Randalstown Road, Antrim BT41 4LJ
Telephone / Fax / e-mail	01849 463535 / 01849 465733
Source	Correspondence.
Notes	#

Nature of Funding	The Trust will consider giving grants for the preservation of religious and secular buildings of historic or architectural interest.
Geographical Area	UK.
Eligible Applicants	Organisations with charitable status only.
Restrictions	No individuals. No grants for "updating" (i.e. installation of modern facilities).
Amount	#
Form of Payment	#
Size of Fund	Medium.
Application Form?	In writing, outlining the project's history, aims, benefit to local community and breakdown of expenditure.
Guidance Notes?	No.
Timetable	Applications are considered at meetings held three times a year.
Contact	The Alan Evans Memorial Trust
Address	The Alan Evans Memorial Trust, Messrs Coutts & Co, Trustee Department, 440 The Strand, London WC2R 0QS
Telephone / Fax / e-mail	0171 753 1269
Source	#
Notes	Applicants will not be advised if their appeal is unsuccessful.

Nature of Funding	Under the Trust's Arts and Heritage programme, it is prepared to consider grant support for the preservation of buildings of historic or architectural value put to public use. (This programme is one amongst five the Trust runs). Grants may be made towards revenue, capital or project expenditure.
Geographical Area	UK.
Eligible Applicants	Organisations with charitable status and religious establishments only. Local and district organisations are particularly encouraged to apply.
Restrictions	No large national charities or their branches. No parish churches. No individuals.
Amount	£250 – £250,000.
Form of Payment	#
Size of Fund	Very large, but see Notes below.
Application Form?	For grants over £5,000, by letter with supporting information. For grants below £5,000, on the Trust's Small Grants Scheme form. All applications are acknowledged.
Guidance Notes?	Yes. Applicants must obtain and follow the Trust's "Guidelines for Applicants".
Timetable	Applications can be made at any time of year and are dealt with within two to six months.
Contact	Judith Dunworth, Trust Secretary
Address	The Esmée Fairbairn Charitable Trust, 7 Cowley Street, London SW1P 3NB
Telephone / Fax / e-mail	0171 227 5400 / 0171 227 5401 / enquiry@esmee-fairbairn.co.uk
Source	#
Notes	Following the sale to Prudential earlier this year of the Trust's major shareholding in M&G the size of its future grantmaking is likely to increase in 2000 and beyond. Trustees will be reviewing their policies over the coming months and expect to decide any changes by the end of 1999. In the meantime existing grantmaking policies will continue to apply.

Nature of Funding	The Trust's main focus is to assist small, isolated communities and isolated neighbourhoods in developing projects of lasting benefit. Projects of an unusual nature are welcomed.
Geographical Area	County Fermanagh.
Eligible Applicants	Local community groups.
Restrictions	No individuals.
Amount	£250 – £5,000 Applications can be made for capital, project and revenue funding. Interest-free loans can be applied for in special circumstances.
Form of Payment	#
Size of Fund	Very small.
Application Form?	By letter, including details of the group and its overall aims. Enclose annual report, audited accounts, outline of project and costings.
Guidance Notes?	Yes.
Timetable	Trustees meet every quarter to consider grant applications. Applications will not be acknowledged unless accompanied by a stamped, addressed envelope.
Contact	The Secretary
Address	The Fermanagh Trust, c/o Rockview, Blacklion, County Cavan, Republic of Ireland
Telephone / Fax / e-mail	00353 72 53010 / 00353 72 53010
Source	#
Notes	The Fermanagh Trust, constituted in 1995, has built on the grant-giving activities of the Barrow Cadbury Trust.

Nature of Funding	The Ford of Britain Trust makes donations to undertakings concerned with the advancement of education and other charitable purposes.
Geographical Area	UK.
Eligible Applicants	Organisations with charitable status only, in close proximity to Ford Motor Company Limited plants in the UK i.e. Belfast.
Restrictions	No individuals. Funding for major building projects is rare.
Amount	£100 – £5,000.
Form of Payment	One-off donations for a specific capital project.
Size of Fund	Small.
Application Form?	By letter, including details of the applicant and their charitable status. Enclose annual report, audited accounts, outline of project and costings.
Guidance Notes?	Yes.
Timetable	The Trustees meet in March, July and November. Applications are considered in order of receipt.
Contact	Mr R M Metcalf
Address	Ford of Britain Trust, Room 1/661, Ford Motor Company Ltd, Eagle Way, Brentwood, Essex CM13 3BW
Telephone / Fax / e-mail	01277 252551
Source	#
Notes	Correspondence.

Nature of Funding	The Trust's principal focus is social welfare, but it will consider giving grants for the preservation of secular buildings of exceptional historic or architectural interest.
Geographical Area	UK.
Eligible Applicants	Organisations with charitable status only.
Restrictions	No individuals or reapplications. No large building projects, general repair work, or projects in receipt of substantial support from other sources. There must be a suitable level of public access.
Amount	Normally £5,000 – £10,000. Some smaller grants of £1,000.
Form of Payment	#
Size of Fund	Very large, but see Notes below.
Application Form?	By letter, no more than two pages long, giving an outline of the project, a cost breakdown, existing sources of finance and other applications for financial assistance.
Guidance Notes?	Yes. These must be obtained and followed before writing in with a request.
Timetable	As every project is visited, it takes at least three months for a grant to be awarded. Smaller grants of up to £1,000 may be awarded without a visit. All applications are acknowledged.
Contact	Ms Bridget O'Brien Twohig
Address	Paul Getty Jr Charitable Trust, 1 Park Square West, London NW1 4LJ
Telephone / Fax / e-mail	0171 486 1859
Source	#
Notes	In 1997 the Trust was only able to support 138 out of 2,157 applications. Grants for heritage/conservation amounted to £90,000. No grants were made in Northern Ireland.

G C Gibson Trust

Nature of Funding	The Trust will consider giving grants for the preservation of religious buildings of historic or architectural interest. Buildings in Scotland or Wales are preferred; those in Suffolk and Herefordshire are also given priority.
Geographical Area	UK.
Eligible Applicants	Organisations with charitable status and religious establishments only.
Restrictions	No individuals.
Amount	£1,000 – £5,000.
Form of Payment	#
Size of Fund	Large.
Application Form?	Applicants should write outlining the nature of their organisation, the project and the need for it. They should enclose copies of their accounts and any associated literature considered relevant, but no video tapes.
Guidance Notes?	No.
Timetable	Meetings to consider applications are held annually in December and cheques are distributed to successful applicants in January. The Trust administrators therefore ask that all applications are submitted by October.
Contact	G C Gibson Trust.
Address	Deloitte & Touche, Blenheim House, Fitzalan Court, Newport Road, Cardiff CF2 1TS
Telephone / Fax / e-mail	01222 481111
Source	#
Notes	#

The Glaziers' Trust

Nature of Funding	Financial assistance for the preservation of important examples of medieval stained and painted glass, post-Reformation glass to the end of the 18th century, and later work of particular historic significance or exceptional artistic merit.
Geographical Area	UK.
Eligible Applicants	Those responsible for the maintenance and restoration of important stained and painted glass in buildings accessible to the public.
Restrictions	Grants are restricted to glass, leading, saddle bars, and fixing. They are not available for stone or brickwork repairs or protection from weather or vandals.
Amount	£300 – £2,500.
Form of Payment	#
Size of Fund	Very small.
Application Form?	On application form, accompanied by a full report, photographs and an estimate from an approved glazier (by whom the work must be carried out).
Guidance Notes?	Yes.
Timetable	The grant is payable when the restoration is completed.
Contact	The Clerk
Address	The Glaziers' Trust, Glaziers' Hall, 9 Montague Close, London SE1 9DD
Telephone / Fax / e-mail	0207 403 3300 / 0207 407 606 / *
Source	#
Notes	Details of historic stained glass available for re-use can be obtained from the Clerk at the address above.

The Grocers' Charity

Nature of Funding	Approximately 200 grants are made annually within a variety of categories, including Arts and the Heritage.
Geographical Area	UK.
Eligible Applicants	Organisations with charitable status and religious establishments only.
Restrictions	No individuals.
Amount	£500 – £5,000.
Form of Payment	Single payment.
Size of Fund	Small.
Application Form?	By letter, including details of the applicant and their charitable status. Enclose annual report, audited accounts, outline of project and costings.
Guidance Notes?	Yes.
Timetable	Applications may be submitted at any time of year and are not acknowledged. The Trustees meet four times a year.
Contact	Miss Anne Blanchard
Address	The Grocers' Charity, Grocers' Hall, Princes Street, London EC2R 8AD
Telephone / Fax / e-mail	0171 6063113 / 0171 6003082
Source	Correspondence.
Notes	Informal telephone enquiries to the Administrator are encouraged.

Idlewild Trust

E18

Nature of Funding	The Trust will consider giving grants for the preservation of religious and secular buildings of historic or architectural interest. It will also support projects involving the preservation of their contents, such as furniture and wall paintings.
Geographical Area	UK.
Eligible Applicants	Organisations with charitable status only.
Restrictions	No individuals. No repetitive nation-wide appeals by large charities. No local appeals. No endowment or deficit funding.
Amount	£2,000 – £3,000.
Form of Payment	#
Size of Fund	Large.
Application Form?	By letter. This should be no longer than two pages of A4 and should describe the applicant organisation, its funding and work and the project, including detailed costs and funding. Enclose a copy of the most recent audited accounts and annual report. Applications are not acknowledged unless a stamped addressed envelope is enclosed.
Guidance Notes?	Yes.
Timetable	Trustees meet three times a year, usually March, July and November. Applications should be submitted four to six weeks before the meeting.
Contact	#
Address	Idlewild Trust, 54–56 Knatchbull Road, London SE5 9QY
Telephone / Fax / e-mail	0171 274 2266 (Tues & Weds 10am – 4pm) / 0171 274 5222
Source	#
Notes	#

Nature of Funding	The Ireland Funds is a composite title for 12 individual funds that seek to promote peace and reconciliation, arts and culture, community development and education. Funding for heritage and conservation is supported if public accessibility to the project is increased.
Geographical Area	Ireland.
Eligible Applicants	Local groups and charities.
Restrictions	No individuals. No funding for the purchase of buildings or land.
Amount	Up to £20,000.
Form of Payment	#
Size of Fund	Very large.
Application Form?	On the application form provided. No accounts to be sent unless requested.
Guidance Notes?	Yes.
Timetable	The Funds accept applications between October and January. As applications are approved by the committee in America, applicants will be contacted by letter the following July. Applicants should not contact the office in the interim period.
Contact	#
Address	The Ireland Funds, No. 5 Foster Place, Dublin 2
Telephone / Fax / e-mail	00353 1 662 7878 / 00353 1 662 7879 / ifdublin@iol.ie
Source	Correspondence.
Notes	For a copy of the guidelines see the web site: www.irlfunds.org

Nature of Funding	The Irish Landmark Trust is NOT a grant making body, but it does acquire buildings of architectural importance which are in need of restoration. Once restored, the property is let as holiday accommodation.
Geographical Area	Ireland.
Eligible Applicants	#
Restrictions	#
Amount	#
Form of Payment	#
Size of Fund	Medium.
Application Form?	#
Guidance Notes?	Yes.
Timetable	#
Contact	The Administrator
Address	The Irish Landmark Trust, 25 Eustace Street, Temple Bar, Dublin 2
Telephone / Fax / e-mail	00353 1 6704733 / 00353 1 6704887
Source	#
Notes	The Irish Landmark Trust does not confine its activities to the restoration of architecturally interesting buildings for holiday letting. It has a strong educational role too, seeking to use local craftsmen, supporting the continuation of traditional skills. In 1998 it conducted a cross border survey of vernacular buildings in counties Cavan, Louth and Sligo.

Nature of Funding	The Fund will consider applications for the restoration of architectural ironwork e.g. gates and grilles. Funding for new forged ironwork by blacksmiths is also considered.
Geographical Area	UK.
Eligible Applicants	Organisations with charitable status and religious establishments only.
Restrictions	No individuals.
Amount	Up to £2,000.
Form of Payment	#
Size of Fund	Small.
Application Form?	By letter including details of the applicant and their charitable status. Enclose annual report, audited accounts, outline of project and costings.
Guidance Notes?	No.
Timetable	The Iron Committee meets annually in May. Applications are requested by March.
Contact	The Administrator
Address	The Ironmongers' Charitable Fund, Ironmongers' Hall, Barbican, London EC2Y 8AA
Telephone / Fax / e-mail	0171 6062725
Source	#
Notes	#

Nature of Funding	The Trust is primarily interested in buildings of the Georgian period. It is prepared to grant aid the preservation of distinct parts of buildings and their contents. It is willing to contribute towards the repair and conservation of church furniture, such as monuments.
Geographical Area	UK.
Eligible Applicants	#
Restrictions	No individuals. No grants for repairs to the fabric of ecclesiastical buildings, or for privately owned properties.
Amount	Average of £1,500 for churches and £5,000 for secular buildings.
Form of Payment	#
Size of Fund	Small.
Application Form?	By letter, describing the applicant and the project. Enclose photographs. All applications will receive a letter either of refusal or offering a grant.
Guidance Notes?	Yes.
Timetable	Trustees meet in February, June and October.
Contact	Mrs L Lawson
Address	The Leche Trust, 84 Cicada Road, London SW18 2NZ
Telephone / Fax / e-mail	0181 870 6233 / 0181 870 6333
Source	#
Notes	#

The Helen Isabella McMorran Charitable Trust E23

Nature of Funding	The Foundation will consider giving grants for the preservation of religious buildings of historic or architectural interest.
Geographical Area	UK.
Eligible Applicants	Organisations with charitable status only. No individuals. Trustees tend to favour applications for specific purposes, events or projects.
Restrictions	#
Amount	£500 – £2,000.
Form of Payment	#
Size of Fund	Medium.
Application Form?	By letter, enclosing any relevant information or reports.
Guidance Notes?	Yes.
Timetable	Trustees meet annually, in March. Applications must be submitted by the end of February.
Contact	The Manager – Charities, The H I McMorran Charitable Foundation
Address	National Westminster Bank Plc, NatWest Investments, 67 Maple Road, Surbiton, Surrey KT6 4QT
Telephone / Fax / e-mail	0181 335 1762
Source	#
Notes	Only successful applicants are notified.

The Manifold Charitable Trust E24

Nature of Funding	The Trust will consider grant aiding the preservation of any buildings of historic or architectural interest.
Geographical Area	UK.
Eligible Applicants	Organisations holding charitable status and religious establishments only.
Restrictions	No individuals.
Amount	Usually £1,000 – £9,000, but no upper limit.
Form of Payment	#
Size of Fund	Very large.
Application Form?	By letter, describing the project with photograph if appropriate, stating the total cost, the amount available from the applicant's own funds and how much has already been received or promised.
Guidance Notes?	No.
Timetable	Applications are considered twice a month. Most applications, apart from circulars, are replied to, usually within three weeks. Successful applicants are notified sooner.
Contact	The Secretary
Address	The Manifold Charitable Trust, Shottesbrooke House, Maidenhead SL6 3SW
Telephone / Fax / e-mail	#
Source	Correspondence with the Trust.
Notes	#

Nature of Funding	The Company will consider giving grants for the preservation of buildings of historic or architectural interest. Grants for religious buildings are not entertained because annual grants are made to central organisations for this purpose.
Geographical Area	UK.
Eligible Applicants	Organisations with charitable status.
Restrictions	No individuals.
Amount	£500 – £3,000.
Form of Payment	#
Size of Fund	Medium.
Application Form?	By letter in the first instance giving outline details and costings.
Guidance Notes?	No.
Timetable	The grant-making committee meets every three months.
Contact	Grants Manager
Address	Mercers' Company, Mercers' Hall, Ironmonger Lane, London EC2V 8HE
Telephone / Fax / e-mail	0171 726 4991 / 0171 600 1158
Source	#
Notes	#

The Esme Mitchell Trust

E26

Nature of Funding	The Trust funds charitable purposes in Ireland as a whole, but principally in Northern Ireland, with particular interest in cultural and artistic objects in Northern Ireland.
Geographical Area	Ireland.
Eligible Applicants	Organisations with charitable status.
Restrictions	Approximately one third of the annual fund is only available to a limited number of heritage bodies.
Amount	No restriction.
Form of Payment	#
Size of Fund	£120,000 per annum (of which approximately one third is only available to a limited number of heritage bodies.
Application Form?	By letter, including details of the applicant and their charitable status. Enclose annual report, audited accounts, outline of project and costings. All the aforementioned information to be submitted in triplicate. The Inland Revenue Charities Division reference number should be sent with the application.
Guidance Notes?	Yes.
Timetable	There is no deadline for applications, which are considered by the Trust Advisers every month.
Contact	The Secretary
Address	Northern Bank Executor and Trustee Company Limited, P O Box 183, Donegal Square West, Belfast BT1 6JS
Telephone / Fax / e-mail	01232 245277 / 01232 241790
Source	Correspondence.
Notes	#

Nature of Funding	Grants towards the preservation of particular features of historic buildings or the conservation of individual monuments or structures of importance to the surrounding environment; projects that give a new use to "outstanding" buildings; dissemination of information about historic buildings and their importance to the community; repair and conservation of architecturally significant churchyard walls and exterior funerary monuments. Capital expenditure preferred. The Trustees are prepared to consider applications that involve salary or other management costs when these have a defined time limit and clear objectives.
Geographical Area	UK.
Eligible Applicants	Organisations with charitable status and religious establishments only.
Restrictions	No individuals. Normally no applications for projects already underway.
Amount	£1,000 – £20,000.
Form of Payment	#
Size of Fund	Very large.
Application Form?	On application form available from the Trust.
Guidance Notes?	Yes.
Timetable	Applications can be made at any time but should arrive at least six weeks before the full board of Trustees' quarterly meeting at which they will be considered.
Contact	Georgina Nayler, Director
Address	The Pilgrim Trust, Fielden House, Little College Street, London SW1P 3SH
Telephone / Fax / e-mail	0171 222 4723 / 0171 976 0461
Source	"Guidelines for Applicants" (The Pilgrims Trust).
Notes	#

Nature of Funding	The Rothschild Foundation will consider giving grants for the preservation of religious and secular buildings of historic or architectural interest.
Geographical Area	UK.
Eligible Applicants	Organisations with charitable status only.
Restrictions	No individuals.
Amount	#
Form of Payment	#
Size of Fund	Very large, but see Notes below.
Application Form?	By letter.
Guidance Notes?	No.
Timetable	#
Contact	The Administrator
Address	The Rothschild Foundation, 14 St James's Place, London SW1A 1NP
Telephone / Fax / e-mail	0171 493 8111
Source	#
Notes	The Trust's funds are heavily committed until the year 2001. Only projects with which the Trustees have a personal connection will be considered until then.

Nature of Funding	Some of the Sainsbury Family Charitable Trusts have supported projects involving the repair and rehabilitation of religious and secular buildings, but in the case of Northern Ireland, probably only The Headley Trust would be applicable. Normally trustees support projects which they have sought out, but unsolicited applications may occasionally be successful.
Geographical Area	UK.
Eligible Applicants	Organisations with charitable status and religious establishments only.
Restrictions	#
Amount	#
Form of Payment	#
Size of Fund	Very large.
Application Form?	By letter, including details of the applicant, the proposed project, its cost and planned outcome. A letter to one trust is considered a letter to all.
Guidance Notes?	No.
Timetable	All applications are acknowledged, but further correspondence takes place only if trustees are able to consider helping.
Contact	Michael Pattison CBE.
Address	Sainsbury Family Charitable Trusts, 9 Red Lion Court, London EC4A 3EF
Telephone / Fax / e-mail	0171 410 0330
Source	Correspondence with Trust.
Notes	Seventeen Sainsbury Family Charitable Trusts are administered from this office, including the Headley Trust, Linbury Trust and Monument Trust.

Shell Better Britain Campaign: Community Projects Fund E30

Nature of Funding	Information, advice and grant aid is offered to community groups with practical projects for improving their local environment, including the condition, appearance and surroundings of buildings.
Geographical Area	UK.
Eligible Applicants	Community groups.
Restrictions	#
Amount	Up to £2,000.
Form of Payment	#
Size of Fund	Small.
Application Form?	On the application form available from Shell Better Britain Campaign. Applicants should pay attention to the sustainability checklist.
Guidance Notes?	Yes.
Timetable	Applications can be made at any time.
Contact	Sarah Betteridge.
Address	Shell Better Britain Campaign, King Edward House, 135a New Street, Birmingham B2 4QJ
Telephone / Fax / e-mail	0121 2485900 / 0121 2485901 / enquiries@sbbc.co.uk
Source	#
Notes	SBBC produces Interactive, an excellent newsletter with much information about sustainable projects and their funding.

The Skinners' Company Lady Neville Charity E31

Nature of Funding	Grants should make a clear and significant contribution to a charitable project or activity. Local heritage is one of the four areas for priority funding. Awards will be for items of non-recurring expenditure only (e.g. capital building works).
Geographical Area	UK.
Eligible Applicants	Organisations with charitable status only.
Restrictions	No individuals.
Amount	£500 – £1,000.
Form of Payment	#
Size of Fund	Very small.
Application Form?	By letter, including details of the applicant and their charitable status. Enclose annual report, audited accounts, outline of project and costings.
Guidance Notes?	Yes.
Timetable	Committees are held in May and November. Applications need to be received four weeks prior to the meeting. Applications are not acknowledged.
Contact	Sue Ellis
Address	The Skinners' Company Lady Neville Charity, Skinners' Hall, 8 Dowgate Hill, London EC4R 2SP
Telephone / Fax / e-mail	0171 2365629 / 0171 2366590
Source	#
Notes	#

The Bernard Sunley Charitable Foundation E32

Nature of Funding	The Foundation gives grants to many causes across a broad range of charitable activities. Amongst these are the preservation of religious and secular buildings of historic or architecture interest.
Geographical Area	UK.
Eligible Applicants	Organisations with charitable status only.
Restrictions	No individuals.
Amount	#
Form of Payment	#
Size of Fund	Very large.*
Application Form?	By letter, with audited accounts and project costings.
Guidance Notes?	#
Timetable	The Foundation notifies successful applicants within three months. It does not inform unsuccessful applicants, but will respond to telephone enquiries two or more months after the application was submitted.
Contact	The Director
Address	The Bernard Sunley Charitable Foundation, 53 Grosvenor Square, London W1X 9FH
Telephone / Fax / e-mail	0171 409 1199 / 0171 409 7373
Source	#
Notes	* Funds are at the moment heavily committed.

Ulster Garden Villages Ltd

Nature of Funding	Ulster Garden Villages Limited was established in 1946 in order to provide good quality housing and associated amenities for the disadvantaged and the aged. Since 1983, the Society has allocated funds to projects within Northern Ireland that will improve the quality of life in the local community. Assisting the restoration of buildings for community use is amongst the objectives.
Geographical Area	Northern Ireland.
Eligible Applicants	Organisations with charitable status only.
Restrictions	No individuals or projects already funded by statutory bodies.
Amount	Normally £1,000 – £2,500, but project assistance up to £250,000 considered.
Form of Payment	#
Size of Fund	Small.
Application Form?	Applications for grants up to £5,000 should be made on the Society's application form which is available on request. Applications for grants over £5,000 should be made by letter including details of the group and its overall aims. Enclose annual report, audited accounts, outline of project and costings.
Guidance Notes?	Yes.
Timetable	Applications may be made at any time.
Contact	The Administration Officer
Address	Ulster Garden Villages Limited, Purdy's Lane, Newtownbreda, Belfast BT8 4AX
Telephone / Fax / e-mail	01232 491111 / 01232 491007
Source	#
Notes	#

The Prince of Wales's Charitable Foundation

Nature of Funding	The Trustees may consider supporting those organisations whose activities seem particularly enterprising in the fields of environment, architecture, heritage and health.
Geographical Area	UK.
Eligible Applicants	Organisations with charitable status only.
Restrictions	No individuals.
Amount	Varies.
Form of Payment	#
Size of Fund	Medium.
Application Form?	By letter, including details of the applicant and their charitable status. Enclose annual report, audited accounts, outline of project and costings.
Guidance Notes?	No.
Timetable	Applications can be made at any time.
Contact	Mr Stephen Lamport
Address	The Prince of Wales's Charitable Foundation, St James Palace, London SW1A 1BS
Telephone / Fax / e-mail	0171 930 4832
Source	Correspondence.
Notes	#

Nature of Funding	The Foundation will consider giving grants for the preservation of religious and secular buildings of historic or architectural interest.
Geographical Area	UK.
Eligible Applicants	Organisations with charitable status and religious establishments only.
Restrictions	No individuals.
Amount	Varies.
Form of Payment	#
Size of Fund	Very large.
Application Form?	By letter, which should contain an outline of the applicant's activities, a synopsis of the proposed project, and details of who will benefit. Enclose the charity's registration number, a copy of its most recent report and audited accounts, the project's financial plan and information about current and proposed fund-raising.
Guidance Notes?	Yes.
Timetable	There is no deadline for applications, which are normally processed within three months of receipt. All applicants are notified of the outcome by letter.
Contact	The Administrator or Secretary to the Trustees
Address	Garfield Weston Foundation, Weston Centre, Bowater House, 68 Knightsbridge, London SW1X 7LQ
Telephone / Fax / e-mail	0171 589 6363
Source	Correspondence with the Foundation.
Notes	#

The Wolfson Foundation   E36

Nature of Funding	The Foundation will consider giving grants for the preservation of religious and secular buildings of historic or architectural interest. Grants are usually for capital expenditure only.
Geographical Area	UK.
Eligible Applicants	Organisations with charitable status and religious establishments only.
Restrictions	No individuals. No grant assistance for the purchase of buildings.
Amount	£2,000 – £20,000.
Form of Payment	#
Size of Fund	Very large.
Application Form?	By letter, which should contain a brief outline of the project, including information on the heritage value of the building or church. Enclose a recent photograph of the site, the envisaged benefits and costs and a copy of the organisation's most recent audited accounts.
Guidance Notes?	#
Timetable	Trustees meet in June and December and applications must be made by the middle of March and the middle of September.
Contact	The Executive Secretary
Address	The Wolfson Foundation, 8 Queen Anne Street, London W1M 9LD
Telephone / Fax / e-mail	0171 323 5730
Source	#
Notes	#

The Woodroffe Benton Foundation E37

Nature of Funding	The Foundation will consider giving grants for the preservation of buildings, both religious and secular, of national historic or architectural interest. Grants are not normally made for projects of local interest only.
Geographical Area	UK.
Eligible Applicants	Organisations with charitable status and religious establishments only.
Restrictions	No individuals.
Amount	Grants do not normally exceed £2,000.
Form of Payment	#
Size of Fund	Large.
Application Form?	By letter. All applications are acknowledged.
Guidance Notes?	Yes.
Timetable	Trustee meetings are held quarterly, in January, April, July, and October. Applications should arrive before the end of the preceding month. Unsuccessful applicants are not notified.
Contact	A F King
Address	The Woodroffe Benton Foundation, 16 Fernleigh Court, Harrow, Middlesex HA2 6NA
Telephone / Fax / e-mail	0181 428 7183
Source	#
Notes	#

World Monument Fund E38

World Monuments Watch

Nature of Funding	World Monuments Fund is the only private charity dedicated to the great monuments of the world. By raising awareness of the need to preserve the global architectural heritage, WMF acts as a catalyst for heritage conservation projects all over the world. World Monuments Watch is not primarily a grant giving foundation, it sees its function as increasing public awareness of an endangered cultural site and advocacy for its preservation.
Geographical Area	World-wide.
Eligible Projects	'Monuments' include palaces, fortifications, temples churches and sometimes whole towns or settlements. Gardens and landscapes are also included. The underpinning of the cliff at Mussenden Temple, Co. Antrim was a recent project. WMW has found that in several cases high profile publicity for a vulnerable site has encouraged the site to be designated and to afford it statutory protection.
Eligible Expenditure	World Monuments Watch maintains a list of the 100 most endangered cultural sites throughout the world.
Restrictions	The World Monuments Fund in Britain cannot fund private projects. Funded sites are usually open to the public. Special circumstances are considered.
Amount	Grants vary according to project. Sites listed on the World Monuments Watch List have received grants of up to $200,000. The Robert Wilson Challenge Programme also matches funds up to £250,000 from non-American donors.
Form of Payment	#
Size of Fund	Large.
Application Form?	There are nomination forms available from the World Monuments Watch List.
Guidance Notes?	#
Timetable	The list is released every two years. Applications available for the 2002 list.
Contact	#
Address	World Monument Watch, 39–40 St James Place, London SW1A 1NS
Telephone / Fax / e-mail	0171 4998254 / 0171 4933982 / wmf@wmf.org.uk
Source	#
Notes	website http://www.worldmonuments.org

Section F

PRIVATE SECTOR SOURCES

Nature of Funding	The Society provides mortgage facilities for projects involving the repair and rehabilitation of derelict or dilapidated buildings and ecological renovation, which often includes traditional building methods.
Geographical Area	UK.
Eligible Applicants	Individuals and co-operatives or other corporate bodies who already have part of the purchase price and earn a living either on the property or from outside employment.
Eligible Projects	#
Eligible Expenditure	#
Restrictions	Maximum loan 80% of valuation.
Amount	Mortgages are subject to an overall limit (details on request). They can be for up to 80% of the valuation or purchase price, whichever is the lower, and are repayable over a 10 to 25 year period. The rate of interest varies. In March 1999 the gross rate was 6.9% for residential property and 9.3% (negotiable) for commercial property.
Form of Payment	Single or multiple tranche (stage payments), depending on project.
Size of Fund	Very large.
Application Form?	Yes.
Guidance Notes?	Yes.
Timetable	Normally within four weeks.
Contact	The Mortgage Department
Address	Ecology Building Society, 18 Station Road, Cross Hills, Near Keighley, West Yorkshire BD20 7EH
Telephone	0845 674 5566
Fax	01535 636166
e-mail	info@ecology.co.uk
Source	"Ecology Mortgages" (The Ecology Building Society).
Notes	#

Mortgages and loans

Nature of Funding	The Bank lends exclusively to projects with clear social and environmental objectives, either mortgages with up to 25 year repayment period or short to medium term loans for periods of one to ten years. The Bank tailors each loan to the specific needs of me borrower and so may be able to provide an arrangement outside of the above terms.
Geographical Area	UK.
Eligible Applicants	The Bank is especially active in the areas of charities, community projects, environmental initiatives and social businesses.
Eligible Projects	See above.
Eligible Expenditure	#
Restrictions	The Bank requires adequate security to be available to support a loan. There are various means of achieving this (contact the Bank for further details).
Amount	Generally between £20,000 and £4 million. Loans are at 1% to 4% above base rate. The Bank normally charges a 1% administration fee on loan offers.
Form of Payment	#
Size of Fund	Very large.
Application Form?	No.
Guidance Notes?	Yes.
Timetable	At the point that the Bank has received all the information required, it will arrange to visit the applicant's premises if this is appropriate. A decision is normally made within one week of the meeting.
Contact	David Cousland
Address	Triodos Bank, Brunel House, 11 The Promenade, Clifton, Bristol BS8 3NN
Telephone	0117 973 9339
Fax	0117 973 9303
e-mail	mail@triodos.co.uk
Source	"Information for borrowers" (Triodos Bank).
Notes	#

SOURCES OF ADVICE
AND USEFUL ADDRESSES

1. NORTHERN IRELAND

Building Preservation Trusts
Advice and information regarding the setting up of a charitable trust:

The Secretary
The UK Association of Building Preservation Trusts (APT)
Clareville House
26/27 Oxendon Street
London SW1Y 4EL

The Phoenix Trust
The Phoenix Trust was launched by its President HRH Prince of Wales in 1997. It is a UK wide Building Preservation Trust with the financial scope to take on larger projects than most local Building Preservation Trusts. It aims to acquire large, unusual and difficult complexes of buildings for sensitive restoration by commercial developers or local BPT's. It welcomes approaches from those disposing of historic estates, including central and local government agencies and private owners.

The United Kingdom Building Preservation Trust
Kit Martin, Park Farm, Gunton Park, Hanworth, Norfolk NR11 7HL
Tel: 01263 761270 Fax: 01263 768642
Email: kitmartin@thephoenixtrust.org.uk

Building Preservation Trusts in Northern Ireland

Northern Ireland Association of Building Preservation Trusts
Secretary: Alison Jones, Elderslie House, 18 Ashley Avenue, BELFAST BT9 7BT
Tel: 01232 665630

Belfast Building Preservation Trust, c/o Fionnuala Jay O'Boyle
Elderslie House, 18 Ashley Avenue, BELFAST BT9 7BT
Tel: 01232 665630

Friends of Lissan Trust, c/o Hazel Radcliffe Dolling,
Lissan House, COOKSTOWN, Co Tyrone, BT80 9SN
Tel: 01648 763312

Galgorm Castle Trust, c/o David J Johnston, Acting Chairman
8 Montgomery Street, GRACEHILL, Co Antrim, BT42 2NN
Tel: 01266 880507/653267 Fax: 01266 881787

Hearth Revolving Fund, c/o Marcus Patton, Director
66 Donegall Pass, BELFAST, BT7 1BU
Tel:01232 530121 Fax:01232 530122

Lecale Building Preservation Trust, c/o Helen Hossack, Secretary
38 Castle Street, KILLOUGH, Co Down, BT30 7QQ
Tel: 01232 660809 Fax: 01232 66175

Mullycovet Mill Project, c/o Sean Burns,
Carra Cottage, Cavanacarragh BELCOO, Co Fermanagh, BT93 5DT
Tel: 01365 386669

Sion Mills Building Preservation Trust c/o Celia Ferguson
Braewood, SION MILLS, Co Tyrone, BT82 9PY
Tel: 028 8165 8224

The Palatine Trust,c/o Helen Hossack, Secretary
38 Castle Street, KILLOUGH, Co Down, BT30 7QQ
Tel: 01232 550213 or 01396 842162 Fax: 01232 550214

Ulster Historic Churches Trust, c/o Carmel McGuckian, Treasurer
1 Ballycregagh Road, Cloughmills, BALLYMENA, Co Antrim BT44 9LD
Tel: 01265 638121 Fax: 01265 638122

Upper Bann Buildings Preservation Trust, c/o Patrick Campbell, Chairman
46 Loughbrickland Road, GILFORD, Co Down BT63 6BN
Tel: 01820 662261 Fax: 01820 628068

Community Technical Aid
Planning and architectural assistance and advice to community groups:

Community Technical Aid
445-449 Ormeau Road
Belfast
BT1 1NB
Tel: 01232 642227
Fax: 01232 642467

Department of Agriculture for Northern Ireland
Statutory responsibility for the Rural Development Programme in Northern Ireland: advice and assistance for farmers and rural landowners:

Countryside Management Division
Department of Agriculture
Dundonald House
Upper Newtownards Road
Belfast
BT4 3SB
Tel: 01232 524713

European Funding
As the funding arrangements for 2000-2006 have not yet been formalised, for the most up to date information contact:

Department of Finance & Personnel
Rosepark House
Upper Newtownards Road
Belfast
Tel: 01232 520400

Once the 2000-2006 funding has been formalised, NICVA European Unit will provide information and advice on how to access European funding and assistance with project development and applications to the various funds:

The European Unit N.I.C.V.A.
127 Ormeau Road
Belfast
BT7 1SH
Tel: 01232 321224
Fax: 01232 438350

The Heritage Lottery Fund
Guidelines, publications offering specialist advice and application forms:

Heritage Lottery Fund
Glendinning House
6, Murray Street
Belfast
BT1 6DN
Tel: 01232 310120
Fax: 01232 310121

Listed Buildings and Historic Building Grants
Information, advice and grant application forms:

Environment & Heritage Service
5-33 Hill Street
Belfast
BTI 2LA
Tel: 01232 235000

The Monuments and Building Record, which contains written information, photographs and drawings relating to historic buildings, structures and archaeological monuments and sites, is at the same address and Telephone number. It is open to the public during office hours, Monday -Friday.

Northern Ireland Council for Voluntary Action and Northern Ireland Voluntary Trust
Support and advice about sources of funding for community based projects:

N.I.C.V.A
Jayne Blayney or Sylvia Gordon
127 Ormeau Road,
Belfast
BT7 ISH
Tel: 01232 321224
Fax: 01232 438350
Email: nicva@nicva.org

N.I.V.T

22 Mount Charles
Belfast
BT7 INZ
Tel: 01232 245972
Tel: 01232 329839

Northern Ireland Housing Executive
Advice and financial assistance:
See the full page advertisement in The Phone Book

The Housing Centre
2 Adelaide Street
Belfast
BT2 8BP
Tel: 01232 240588

Planning Offices
Contact for information about Planning issues, Urban Development Grant and Conservation Areas.

Planning Service Headquarters
Clarence Court
10-18 Adelaide Street
Belfast
BT2 8GB
Tel: 01232 540540
Fax: 01232 540665

Ballymena Divisional Planning Office	Tel: 01266 653333 Fax: 01266 662127
Belfast Divisional Planning Office	Tel: 01232 252800 Fax: 01232 252828
Craigavon Divisional Planning Office	Tel: 01762 341144 Fax: 01762 341065
Coleraine Sub-Divisional Planning Office	Tel: 01265 41300 Fax: 01265 41434
Downpatrick Divisional Planning Office	Tel: 01396 612211 Fax: 01396 618196
Enniskillen Sub-Divisional Planning Office	Tel: 01365 327270 Fax: 01365 328016
Londonderry Divisional Planning Office	Tel: 01504 319900 Fax: 01504 319777
Omagh Divisional Planning Office	Tel: 01662 242881 Fax: 01662 244253

Rural Development Council for Northern Ireland and Rural Community Network
Advice and assistance for community and voluntary groups involved with rural regeneration projects:

Rural Development Council
Loy Street
Cookstown, Co Tyrone
BT80 8PE
Tel: 016487 66980
Fax: 016487 66922

Rural Community Network
45 James Street
Cookstown, Co Tyrone
BT80 8AA
Tel: 016487 66670
Fax: 016487 66006

The Sacred Land project
The Sacred Land project is five year joint venture between WWF-UK and the International Consultancy on Religion, Education and Culture (ICOREC), involving all major religions and conservation groups. Launched in 1997, its aim is to involve people across the UK in conserving, enhancing and developing sacred sites. The Sacred Land project is NOT a funding body, not is it involved in the preservation of buildings, but it is a possible route for the conservation of churchyards, memorials and gravestones.
The Sacred Land Project is co-ordinating with the Shell Better Britain Campaign - Community projects (see E 31,p.60)

Sacred Land Skill Bank
3 Wynnstay Grove
Manchester
M14 6XG
Tel: 0161 2485731

Sources for Railways
The Railway Heritage Trust operates in England Wales and Scotland as an independent registered company limited by guarantee. It is sponsored by Railtrack PLC and Rail Property Ltd.
There is no equivalent body operating in Ireland although there are several excellent railway centres and museums
The main source of funding for the restoration of rail transport related buildings would be from the Heritage Lottery Fund: Industrial, Transport and Maritime Projects.

For further information contact:

The Chairman
The Heritage Railway Association
The Sidings
66 Richmond Court
Lisburn
Co Antrim
BT27 4QX

The Ulster Architectural Heritage Society
Advice and information on architectural and planning matters:

Ulster Architectural Heritage Society
66 Donegall Pass
Belfast
BT7 1BU
Tel: 028 9055 0213
Fax: 028 9055 0214

2.   FUNDING ADVICE

Charities Aid Foundation
Publications on sources of funds and fundraising:

> Charities Aid Foundation
> Kings Hill
> West Malling
> Kent
> ME19 4TA
> Tel: 01732 520000

Directory of Social Change
Publications on source of funds and fundraising

> Directory of Social Change
> 24 Stephenson Way
> London
> NW1 2DP
> Tel: 0171 2095151

Funderfinder
Database of funding sources which allows users to undertake specific sources. To find local access point contact:

> Funderfinder
> 65 Raglan Road
> Leeds
> LS2 9DZ
> Tel: 0113 243 3008

Grant tracker
N.I.C.V.A. is currently compiling a computerised database of funds, contact:

> N.I.C.V.A
> Jayne Blayney or Sylvia Gordon
> 127 Ormeau Road
> BT7 1SH
> Tel: 01232 321224
> Fax: 01232 438350
> Email: nicva@nicva.org

Business in the Community
Advice on possible business sponsorship:

> Business in the Community
> c/o PK-ECC Ltd
> 770 Upper Newtownards Road
> Belfast
> BT16 0UL
> Tel: 01232 410410

3.   SOURCES OF INFORMATION: British Isles

Civic Trust
17 Carlton House Terrace, London SW1Y 4AW
Tel: 0171 0300914

English Heritage
23 Savile Row, London W1X 1AB
Tel: 0171 9733000

The Georgian Group
6 Fitzroy Square, London WIP 6DN
Tel: 0171 3871720

The Irish Georgian Society
74 Merrion Square, Dublin 2
Tel: 003531 6620290

Living over the Shop
Anne Petherick, University of York, The King's Manor,
York YOI 2EP
Tel: 01904 433972

SAVE Britain's Heritage
77 Cowcross Street, London ECIM 6BP
Tel: 0171 2533500

Society for the Protection of Ancient Buildings
37 Spital Square, London EI 6DY
Tel: 0171 3771644

The Twentieth Century Society
77 Cowcross Street, London ECIM 6BP
Tel: 0171 2533500
The Victorian Society
I Priory Gardens, Bedford Park, London W4 ITT
Tel: 0181 9941019

4. BIBLIOGRAPHY

Funds for Historic Buildings in England and Wales
A directory of Funds
Architectural Heritage Fund   1998.1999

A Directory of sources of financial assistance for Historic Buildings in Northern Ireland
Christopher Colville & Elaine Grey (draft manuscript)

Funding for Voluntary Action- a guide to local trusts in Northern Ireland
Northern Ireland Voluntary Trust 1998

Sources of financial assistance for Historic Buildings in Scotland
Scottish Civic Trust   1998

Cultural Directory for Northern Ireland 1999/2000
Cultural Management Training Programme Board

A guide to the Major Trusts vol.1 1999/2000
Directory of Social Change

The Directory of Grant Making Trusts
Focus Series: Environment, Animal welfare and Heritage
Charities Aid Foundation

INDEX

Index

Photographs

Front cover: The Chapel of the Resurrection, off the Antrim Road, Belfast.
          Featured in Buildings at Risk, vol. 3. This project is shortly to be undertaken by the Belfast Building Preservation Trust, with assistance from the
          Architectural Heritage Fund.

Back cover: 9-12 College Square North, Belfast. Featured in Buildings at Risk, vol. 1. Before and after restoration by Hearth Housing Association, with
          financial assistance from the Heritage Lottery Fund.

          Clonard House, off the Falls Road. Featured in Buildings at Risk, vol. 3. Before restoration by Oakleigh Housing Association.

          Curry's Cottage, Derrylin, Co. Fermanagh. Restoration by Hearth Revolving Fund with financial assistance from the Heritage Lottery Fund and the
          Environment & Heritage Service.

          Meeting Street, Dromore. On the Buildings at Risk database. To be restored as part of the Heritage Lottery Townscape Heritage Initiative.

          Former Court House, Markethill, Co. Armagh. Featured in Buildings at Risk, vol. 1.
          Restored by Consarc Conservation with funding from the International Fund for Ireland, the Heritage Lottery Fund, Armagh City & District
          Council, the Partnership Board for Peace and Reconciliation and the Environment & Heritage Service.